English Whisky

THE JOURNEY FROM
GRAIN TO GLASS

English Whisky

TED BRUNING &
RUPERT WHEELER

PAVILION

Dedicated to the memory of James Nelstrop, founder of the English Whisky Company

First published in 2024 by Pavilion, an imprint of
HarperCollins Publishers Ltd
1 London Bridge Street
London SE1 9GF
www.harpercollins.co.uk

HarperCollins Publishers
1st Floor, Watermarque Building
Ringsend Road Dublin 4
Ireland

10 9 8 7 6 5 4 3 2 1

ISBN 978-0-00-862155-1

Publishing Director: Laura Russell
Produced and conceived by Posthouse Publishing, www.posthousepublishing.com
Commissioning Editor: Ellen Simmons
Project Editor: Fiona Holman
Designer: Lily Wilson
Senior Production Controller: Grace OByrne
Cover designer: Georgina Hewitt
Cover Image: Steve Jenkins
Printed and bound by GPS in Bosnia Herzegovina

www.pavilionbooks.com

Pages 2–3 A copita tasting glass, bung and cask at The Lakes distillery.

CONTENTS

FOREWORD

By Dan Szor, founder and managing director of Cotswolds Distillery

In a business where time is measured in decades, centuries and generations, the growth in the English whisky sector is amazing to behold. When I opened the Cotswolds Distillery in 2014 we were the fourth whisky distillery in England in over a hundred years. At time of writing there are nearly 50 English whisky distilleries producing several million litres of English whisky every year, and by 2024 the value of casked English whisky is expected to surpass £1 billion. I recently viewed the self-described largest private collection of English whisky bottlings in the world, which at present counts nearly 500 unique bottlings and is growing every month!

How and why was this industry able to mobilise and grow so quickly? The boom in craft distilling seen in the USA, with over 2,000 distilleries set up in the past 15 years, provided significant proof of concept to those like myself who had an idea to open in the UK. When the craft-distilling revolution arrived in the UK it focused far more on gin, which was undergoing a revitalisation thanks to iconic brands like Bombay and Hendricks. The choice of gin was perhaps due also to the financially more challenging context for whisky-making in the UK and Europe where spirit must be aged for a minimum of three years, versus the USA where there is no legal minimum ageing requirement.

The reluctant agreement by Her Majesty's Revenue & Customs to allow small stills (traditionally forbidden to be below 1,800 litres) opened the floodgates to micro-distillers of gin and other spirits on a manageable scale. While this was happening, a few intrepid entrepreneurs – guided either by a dream such as me or, in the case of Adnams by significant brewing capacity – began laying down casks of whisky. The availability of malt was important as was a culture of alcohol production and brand-building (and investment appetite) in England which made it as good a place as any to make whisky. It should be noted that this has not occurred in isolation: the growth of small-scale whisky production has been unabated across Europe and indeed around the world.

Many of the new English whisky distilleries have taken on the character of their regions as a way to highlight the uniqueness of their offerings, and quite a few are based in beautiful parts of the country, from the Lake District to the Cotswolds, from Cornwall to the Yorkshire Dales. Others are in urban areas and have built their image around a hip cocktail vibe. Most of them offer and count on visitors for high-margin revenue and brand-building. Some are happy to stay micro while others have developed a more ambitious plan to be national, and even international brands. Most have focused on the premium sector where margins are higher and recent category growth has been strongest. Many have also focused on other spirits, in particular gin, as a means of helping cashflow during the painful early years while their whisky matures.

Whisky-making is a financially punishing business model for a start-up involving both significant CapEx and ongoing working capital to lay down stocks for many years. Equally punishing is the cost of building a consumer brand, which requires physical availability, share of mind and trial – factors which are extremely difficult to create and maintain. There will therefore undoubtedly be distilleries who decide or are forced, to abandon their journey because of lack of sales, funds or both. As punishing a business as it may be, however, there is continued interest from 'flavour explorers', who typically drink less but better, and who look for true authenticity and provenance. The premium spirits category, particular brown spirits, continues to outperform and there is a great interest in the collectability and investment potential of whisky.

People often ask me 'what an English whisky tastes like' as if one could readily attribute a national character to our product – something I believe is impossible in most categories of spirit. What does a Scotch whisky taste like? It would depend on the distillery, the process, the wood programme, the business plan. In my view, the most defining element shared by English whisky makers is their youth, vibrancy, independence, commitment to creativity and desire to make a great and differentiated product. This is not 'PLC' whisky, as I sometimes refer to it, but rather an interesting independent spirit. And as punishing a business as it is, the chance to make a beautiful product and create a legacy is a heady drug and one which in my opinion will keep English whisky growing in years to come.

INTRODUCTION
How England is becoming a land of malt & honey

When I started this book, the big question about English whisky was: 'What even is it?' Now, the question has changed to: 'Where is it on sale? I want some!' Well, it's top-shelf stuff that probably won't be coming to a supermarket near you overnight; but what with the speed at which the supplier base is growing, I'd say you are likely to see English whisky being stocked in all major supermarkets soon.

There should be little reason for surprise at English whisky's emergence, especially when artisan distilling generally has hit such an expansive and creative phase. This has been particularly true of whisky distilling. The dominance of UK artisan distilling by gin and vodka is waning. More and more new entrants to the craft are opting to produce darker spirits – rum, brandy or whisky – for despite Russian adventurism, Covid, climate change and whatever unknowable future crises, there is a global shortage of whisky looming. The world's nouveaux riches – Brazil, Russia, India and China (or BRICs) – are drinking their way through the stuff so steadily that mature stocks are already running low. At the time of writing some 30 new malt distilleries, some of them enormous, as well as extensions to existing sites are at various stages of development in Scotland itself; many more are being built around the world. Given the growth in world demand, it may well be that the whole focus of England's craft distilling boom switches from gin to whisky in the next few years.

Indeed, it turns out that many artisanal distillers had whisky in mind from the off and only diverted their attention to gin for the cash flow. For the truth is that whisky has been a product entirely suited to England's topography and climate all along, but that in a capital-intensive economy you need a return on your investment yesterday and you can't afford to allow your product to take its time. The enshrining in law 120-odd years ago of the three-year minimum maturation period that qualified a spirit to call itself whisky was originally a food safety measure intended to prevent the adulteration of malt whisky by mixed-grain spirits produced on continuous stills. If both types of spirit had to be matured in oak for three years, it was argued the taint of grain as cheap padding would be to some extent vitiated. And so it has proved, for the requirement that came into being as a penal measure is now touted as a hallmark of quality.

This is in some ways a crucial moment for English whisky. The legacy European Union regulations defining whisky's identity have run out, and the Government has been mulling their replacement.

In its lobbying on the subject the English Whisky Guild has urged that the three-year rule be retained; and with the mighty Scotch Whisky Association also in favour, the odds are that the status quo will survive. This, however, rather tends to undermine those more progressive souls in the industry who have followed the lead of the late Dr Jim Swan, the Einstein of Distilling, in finding ways to shorten the maturation period (and cost) without loss of quality. It looks increasingly as though they will be told that, by all means, continue bottling your product at two years old, but don't expect to be allowed to start calling it whisky. It may be that a continued insistence on the narrow definition leads to the word disappearing altogether. It's hard to tell so early in the game how this potential rift between the three-year sticklers and the iconoclasts will be resolved; We live, as ever, in interesting times!

Not only interesting times, but exciting too. When researching this book I have often found myself excited by this particular discovery or that particular innovation. For instance, I was made absurdly happy by Christian Jensen of Bermondsey distillery's investment in establishing a cooperage in North Yorkshire, thereby salvaging the careers of two brewer's coopers – Alistair Simms and Jason Manby, almost the last two in England – and at the same time reviving, Phoenix-like, an entire trade that was once essential and ubiquitous.

This is an oft-repeated pattern in any field that embraces artisans. In craft distilling as in microbrewing, in just about any branch of food and drink manufacture, and for all I know in every branch of every other trade and craft, once you let the artisans loose they have an energising and transformative effect. No tradition is sacred, for even when they do follow tradition they often reinvent them in their own way. They create jobs as they grow, rather than growing via merger and takeover and concentration and rationalisation. And here, in English whisky, they have taken what went before and changed it into something rich and strange.

The tasting notes in the Gazetteer have been very kindly furnished by the independent on-line wine and spirit merchants, Masters of Malt, whose permission to plagiarise I decided to beg for because once I took on a tasting of 18 different samples of Calvados and lost. The tasting notes supplied cannot, alas, be comprehensive because artisan distillers have a habit of making single casks, small batches, limited editions and so forth, so not all their products exist all the time. Nevertheless we hope the notes attached here are informative and entertaining. Masters of Malt can also, of course, supply you with whatever takes your fancy.

LLEWELLINS & JAMES,

Castle Green, BRISTOL,

Manufacturers of all descriptions of Distillers', Brewers' & Refiners' Plant & Machinery

ARCHITECTS, ENGINEERS, COPPERSMITHS, BELLFOUNDERS, &c.

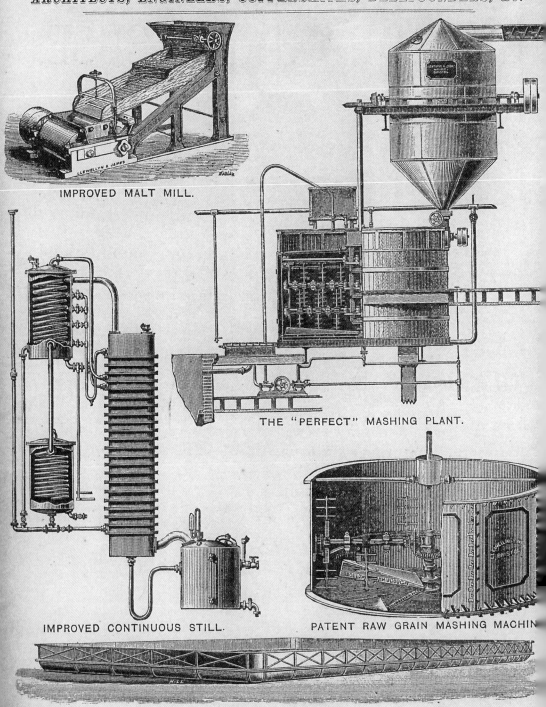

IMPROVED MALT MILL.

THE "PERFECT" MASHING PLANT.

IMPROVED CONTINUOUS STILL.

PATENT RAW GRAIN MASHING MACHIN

CAST IRON COOLER.

CHAPTER ONE

THE WHISKY TRADITIONS

LEARNING FROM ISLAM

'The medicinal spirit was known throughout the west as *aqua vitae*, water of life; and transliterated in the wild Gaelic west as *uisquebaugh*.'

Advertisment from The Whisky Distilleries of the United Kingdom by Alfred Barnard and first published in 1887.

Whisky is Scottish. Whiskey with an 'e' is Irish or American. Gin is English. We all know that. But don't you just hate it when all your certainties fall apart? Because none of it is strictly true. Whisky is, in fact, Persian. So let's step back to late eighth-century Persia, where the Father of Chemistry, Jabir ibn Hayyan (d. 815), was the first experimenter to try evaporating wine. Why? Well, it was a nice day, he hadn't got much else on, and anyway why not? Jabir noticed that when boiled with salt, wine produced a flammable vapour; but until a successor of his came up with an enclosed apparatus to condense the vapour and collect the condensates it wasn't much of a big deal. With a condenser attached, it became a very big deal indeed.

Jabir and the other alchemists of the Arab Enlightenment didn't invent distillation, of course: the salt that made continued human existence possible was mostly produced by distillation; metals were separated from their ores by processes based on the principles of distillation; and all over the interconnected world of the Hellenised Middle East essential oils were separated by distillation from their precursor herbs and flowers to produce all sorts of cosmetics and medicines. But in the alcohol discovered by those early medieval Persian experimenters the world found it had a solvent of previously unimagined versatility: a flammable, even explosive, instrument of war and destruction; or a soothing and aromatic instrument of health and wholeness. Or, of course, a belting night out.

The new miracle product soon crossed the sea from Islamic North Africa to the old-established medical school in Salerno and other similar institutions, especially in Spain, where generations of monastic infirmarers, the pharmacists of their day, came from all over western Christendom to learn their trade. They in turn took the science back to their infirmaries, where warm infusions or even redistilled compounds of healing herbs, diluted and perhaps sweetened for potability, improved if not medical outcomes at least the quality of whatever remained of their patients' lives. That the spirits made by the monastic infirmarers were intended as medicines is evidenced by their small-scale distillation on table-top retorts and by the comparatively expensive base alcohol the monks always used – wine. Not until in the fourteenth century did the monks of northern Europe turn instead to their native and of course much cheaper malt liquors for the base alcohol, an innovation that detracted not at all from the efficacy of their potions but added handsomely to the funds available for the almoner's charitable disbursements. Whether made of wine or malt and whether compounded with herbs or administered plain, the medicinal spirit was known throughout the west as *aqua vitae*, water of life; abbreviated in Russia, Poland and all points east as vodka, or little water; and transliterated in the wild Gaelic west as *uisquebaugh*.

Fast forward now to 1 June 1494 and we find in the Scottish Exchequer Rolls a bill of sale to one Brother John Cor of Lindores Abbey for eight bolls of malt with which to make *aqua vitae*. This document is always portrayed as whisky's birth certificate. It is nothing of the sort. You will have been told it so often that you doubtless believe it, but the truth is that we are still some 300 years from anything you would recognise as whisky.

THE GAELIC TRADITIONS

One of the most famous and yet most misinterpreted Latin sentences in the history of alcohol, the Exchequer Roll entry actually reads: *Et per liberacionem factam Fratri Johanni Cor per preceptum compotorum rotulatoris, ut asserit, de mandato domini regis ad faciendum aquavite… viij bolle brasii* or: 'Delivery has been made to Brother John Cor, on the order of the Comptroller as he has reported (and) by mandate of the lord king… of eight bolls of malt for making *aqua vitae*'. So, then: not whisky's birth certificate but closer, if anything, to that of gin. For what the learned infirmarers needs his eight bolls for is the distillation of pure alcohol (or as pure as he can get it, which was probably not very) as a base for medicinal tinctures as above and, possibly, the alchemical experiments of which James IV was so fond. A 'boll' was a dry measure whose weight fluctuated vastly according to when and where it was cited: according to a trade almanac of 1863 it amounted to 320lb of barley, so Friar John's allowance might have come to as much as 2,560lb or 1.15 tons – enough to make 3,852 litres of wash at 8 per cent abv or thereabouts or, after going through the still twice, 350-odd litres of pure(ish) alcohol.

That's not actually a huge amount: even liquored down by half it wouldn't have kept the court merry for very long. But what Brother John was making was a malt-based clear spirit pretty much identical to those made by abbey infirmarers and, increasingly, lay apothecaries all over north-western Europe. It was not intended as a beverage but both as a curative and as a fortifying preventive, as witness the fact that it was served in drams of about half the capacity of a modern teaspoon. It has been observed that eight bolls of malt might not make much whisky but would make a powerful lot of cough mixture; but as well as serving its own community and possibly the royal court too, Lindores – a large and prominent establishment founded and endowed by the mighty Leslie family – controlled more than 30 daughter houses and lay parishes. That's a powerful lot of coughs!

WHISKY FAR AND WIDE

It seems from these recipes and in particular from the spices common to many of them and references that as late as the early nineteenth century *usquebaugh*, but for the absence of juniper, was still closer to gin than to whisky, possessing few if any of the characteristics that define whisky today and which come from long keeping in oak barrels. Oak has several properties that tend to soften and mellow the harsh raw spirit, which we shall come to later; and it is porous, allowing some of the ethanol to evaporate and further blunt the spirit's edge. But it takes time for these properties to take effect, and for this mystical union we have to thank not pious Brother John but all those Highland farmers who, by the mid-sixteenth century, had already hit on preservation by distillation as the best way of protecting grain prices against the fluctuations of the weather.

James IV, as well as patronising Brother Cor, also issued a charter in 1505 granting a partial monopoly on distilling in and around Edinburgh to the city's surgeon barbers, allowing the necessary skills to break out of the cloister and filter through the wider community. Highland farmers, who soon picked up the necessary skills, were in large part transhumant herdsmen who drove their cattle up into the hills to graze throughout the summer and then, as the upland pickings thinned out, drove them back down into the glens to perform one last and most important task before winter closed in. Once those selected for salting had been slaughtered, those chosen to live were turned out into the little cornlands, now harvested, before being committed to their winter quarters. Here the cattle would get one last hearty feed on the stubble while manuring the ground, turning and treading the soil to a soft, deep, easily worked tilth ready for the spring barley, and breaking up the root systems of pernicious weeds to stop them regrowing after the winter frost had thawed. (The cattle preferred barley stubble to wheat because barley straw is softer, which also makes it more suitable than wheat straw for animal bedding.) But even such careful husbandry could not guarantee regular harvests, and while the scarcity occasioned by the bad harvests might be matched by the surplus from the good, prices fell in glut years and the farmer's family was no better off. Distilling was the answer to their prayers. Surplus malt, brewed and then sealed into the household's wash (and brewing) copper fitted with a tight lid and a little flue pipe and set on a very carefully watched fire (borrowing a skill essential in brewing), yielded an imperishable liquor that would fetch a good price from the apothecaries in town (however distant that might be) in the next poor year. The spirit was stored from year to year, or even over a number of years, in oak casks, which meant it could be held back until prices recovered.

And then someone – or more likely several people at once – made the discovery that gave us whisky as we know and love it. It is to be supposed that pharmacists were at first the principal buyers of the farmers' raw spirit. But great houses would lay in a stock too, to compound their own nostrums. And, too, the farming communities themselves would commonly start their days with a fortifying dram of pure, unrectified, oak-aged whisky discovering, along with the chronicler Raphael Holinshead, how 'being moderately taken, it slows the age, it cuts phlegm, it lightens the mind, it quickens the spirit, it cures the dropsy, it heals the strangulation, it pounces the stone, its repels gravel, it pulls away ventositie, it keeps and preserves the head from whirling, the eyes from dazzling, the tongue from lisping, the mouth from snuffling, the teeth from chattering, the throat from rattling, the weasan from stiffing, the stomach from womblying, the heart from swelling, the belly from wincing, the guts from rumbling, the hands from shivering, the sinews from shrinking, the veins from crumpling, the bones from aching, (and) the marrow from soaking.' In short, just what you need on a cold and frosty Highland morning. And delicious with it.

A NOBLE BIRTH ACKNOWLEDGED

The travails and tribulations of whisky distilling in Scotland after excise duty was introduced in 1643 belong to another book. Suffice it to say that gaugers and bothiemen chased each other up ben and down glen until 1823 when pressures from all directions – commercial, social, cultural, political and gastronomical – came to a head and the whole business was settled by an uncommonly sensible set of compromises. This probably had a lot to do with the fact that George IV acquired a keen taste for it, having been given a glass of Glenlivet at a ball during his visit to Edinburgh in 1822; but he was not the first of the gentry to discover malt whisky's glories; and it was from the Anglophone gentry of Edinburgh and the south-east of Scotland (Anglophone not because of southern incomers, but because the British kingdom of Bryneich, modern Berwickshire and Lothian, had been overrun by Angles centuries before) that the dram acquired its modern name, an Anglicised abbreviation of the Gaelic: whisky.

THE ENGLISH TRADITION

That England has no tradition of whisky distilling is, when you look around you, glaringly obvious. If we ever did have one, it would surely have left a trace visible to anyone with even a casual interest. But no bottle-collector of the author's acquaintance – and there have been a few – has ever proudly showed off a green-tinted 1876 Harrogate Finest Old 26oz case-bottle in mint condition because there never was such a thing, label slightly foxed or otherwise. And yet, and yet. The progress of the distilling industries in England and Scotland after their various Reformations are remarkably similar, and had it not been for the misleading interpolation of the Gaelic word usquebaugh they would hardly have been distinguishable at all. Ireland's Reformation and the progress of its distilling industry diverge wildly from Britain's and are not part of the story of English whisky.

English monks and apothecaries had as long a tradition of making and writing about the distillation of wine as any of their Continental counterparts. Adelard of Bath takes us back to the early decades of the twelfth century; the Compendium Medicinae of Gilbertus Anglicus (c1180–1250) takes the use of *aqua vitae* or *aqua ardens* in medicine as a given; the British Library's Sloan Collection MS964 attributes the late reawakening of the sexual appetite of Queen Isabella (d. 1358), wife and betrayer of Edward II and mother of Edward III, to an elixir distilled from the lees of strong wine and infused with cloves, ginger, nutmeg, gallingale, cubebs, grains of Paris, long pepper, black pepper, caraway, cumin, fennel, parsley, sage, mint, rue and oregano; and Henry VI's Master of Stillatories or court apothecary Robert Broke (1432–55) oversaw the replacement of earthenware in distilling equipment with glass. Fragments of glass alembics regularly turn up in architectural digs at abbeys across Britain, and references to the purchase and use of distilling equipment by monastery infirmarers are equally commonplace. But all these worthies worked with wine, for England was awash with it and remained so throughout the Tudor period. Its southern and western ports had been vastly important emporia for the international wine trade since the late twelfth century. The strong and sweet Iberian and Mediterranean wines beloved of Falstaff and his drinking companions left little room in the market for spirits, while the peasantry enjoyed strong beers such as 'double double', brewed from the finest and most plentiful barley in the world, which didn't need distilling to produce cheerful oblivion. So the apothecaries could easily and cheaply satisfy their medicinal and alchemical requirements with spirits generally distilled from sour wines or wine lees.

The loss of Gascony in 1453 put an abrupt and final end to the 300-year-old Angevin Empire, which had supplied England with all the wine it could drink. At the same time, however, the reconquest of Iberia from Muslim control was almost complete, and the vineyards that had for so long produced mainly sugar-rich table grapes needed new markets. Affluent English wine-drinkers had to change their tastes, since the port, the Canary, the sherry (or sack) and the Malmsey also immortalised by Shakespeare were sweeter, stronger and heavier than the table wines of Bordeaux and the Loire. Even though these wines were not yet fortified, a development that was not widely adopted until the late seventeenth century, they satisfied demand for a stronger, higher-status drink than ale or beer and thus held back the rise to market dominance of malt spirits. Elizabethan trade and technical literature, spread into every field of endeavour through the ubiquity of the printing press, gives us a rough idea of when it finally occurred. These manuals included two entirely separate translations of the Treasure of Euonymus published in 1552 by the Swiss doctor, botanist, zoologist and general polymath Conrad Gessner, known in his lifetime as the Swiss Pliny. Peter Morwyng's translation went to three editions within a year of its publication in 1565; the version by George Baker, *The Newe Jewell of Health*, followed shortly and was more successful still. One of Gessner's recommendations was that a base of spoilt wine or wine lees should be preferred over sound wine. As *The Newe Jewell* has it: 'The burning water, or water of life, is sometimes distilled out of pleasant and good wine, as the white or the red, but oftener out of the wine lees of a certain eager-savour or corrupt Wine. Further, when out of pure wine a water of life is distilled, I hear that out of a great quantity of good wine, a little yield or quantity of burning water is to be distilled, but out of the lees of wine, a much (greater) yield and quantity (are) gathered.' Morwyng's take on the same passage includes the insight that the sale of lees to distillers was a highly profitable sideline for wine merchants: 'Burning-water, or *aqua vitae*,' he writes, 'is drawn oute of wyne, but, wyth us, out of the wyne lies only, specially of them that sel it, and by this onely almost get their livying. And peradventure it is never a whit the worse that it is drawne oute of lees; for Lullus teacheth that it may be wel destilled of corrupt wine, yea, if it be distilled often it shal be made the more effectuall (that is to say), hotter and drier, etc.' But even as these volumes were roaring off the presses, across the North Sea events were unfolding that would see wine-based spirits toppled by malt.

As a semi-autonomous province of Burgundy the late medieval States General – modern Holland and Belgium and the Flemish-speaking county of France north of Calais – had access to the vineyards of Burgundy and Flanders, and to imports from Spain. In the late fifteenth century a long series of wars led to the Spanish taking control of the whole region; but in 1585 the seven northernmost provinces – effectively, modern Holland – broke away, isolating the Dutch from their supplies of Spanish wine. This had far-reaching consequences, for the people of the Low Countries' thickly clustered and prosperous cities had been acquiring a taste for brandy – indeed, the Dutch coined the word *brandewijn* – and several cities had developed thriving distilling industries. The burghers of the breakaway provinces therefore fell back on two expedients. One was to lend money to the winemakers of the Charente in south-west France to enable them to set up as distillers, thus founding the cognac industry; the second was to pad out the precious wine in their wash with malt liquor. Quite soon an all-malt spirit infused with various medicinal herbs became the norm among ordinary citizens, while the rich stuck to their cognac. This malt liquor, apart from the choice of herbs, was almost exactly the same product as *usquebaugh*, even down to storage in oak, and its modern descendant still shows a family resemblance. Not everyone was happy with the change: many late sixteenth-century writers protested at the diversion of grain from its proper purpose of breadmaking and decried malt brandy (for so they called it) as being vastly inferior to the original. Perhaps they had shares in cognac? At any rate, their protests were unheeded: the bourgeoisie had found a product perfectly suited both to palate and wallet and stuck with it. That they called both products brandy adds a layer of confusion for us today, and to make matter worse malt brandy, which was close to whisky, was soon to be reinvented as gin.

The English started developing their own aromatised malt brandy – again, almost identical to *usquebaugh* – as a result of regular commercial, cultural and military contact (both alongside and against) with the Dutch over many generations throughout the sixteenth and seventeenth centuries; and given that variously herbalised malt-based spirits were by now predominant in Scandinavia (akvavit), Germany (kornbrand) and the Slavic lands (vodka, or more accurately, protovodka) as well as Scotland and Ireland, you might plausibly argue that the whole of Northern and Eastern Europe was a single contiguous malt land whose national spirits were very nearly identical.

EARLY DISTILLING

Meanwhile, there is evidence that small-scale artisan distilling was beginning to emerge in England, not so much after the Irish and Scottish model of farmers adding shelf-life and value to glut harvests, but along lines that were to become a very typical feature of the English pub: as extensions to existing retail businesses. Peter Clark, in *The English Alehouse: A Social History 1200–1830*, records a pub called the Aqua Vitae House in Barking in 1572, three such operations licensed in Salisbury in 1584, and a customer asking to be allowed to have a little lie-down after trying the *aqua vitae* made by Goody Streat at her alehouse in East Grinstead. The trade was apparently substantial enough in the 1590s for two businessmen, Robert Drake and Michael Stanhope, to buy a royal monopoly granting them the right to licence all distilleries in England making 'aquacomposita, aquavitie, beere vinegar, or allegar... to be sould or put to sale' for a term of 21 years. In April 1600 we find their deputy Gerson Willford licensing William Catcher of the Red Lion, East Smithfield, to brew ale or beer for the purpose of distillation and sell the spirit in London, Westminster and Southwark at a licence fee of 6d a barrel. The patent was evidently not as profitable as Drake and Stanhope had expected, since it lapsed in 1601. But malt spirit was catching on: Hugh Plat in *Delights for Ladies* (1609) includes a section entitled Secrets of Distillation comprising 25 spirit-based recipes, all for medicines and cosmetics except a 'very principal aqua composita', which includes balm, rosemary flowers, dried red rose leaves, penny-royal, elecampane root, 'the whitest that can be got', liquorice, cinnamon, mace, galingale, coriander seeds, caraway seeds, nutmeg, aniseed, and borage; all finely chopped, steeped in ale for a day and night, and distilled. This, says Markham, 'was made for a learned physician's own drinking;' and if its battery of 14 botanicals seems a little inflated, well, there are artisan gins being concocted today that are just as elaborate.

By the 1620s London had around 200 distilleries, selling much of their output as ship's stores which crews could fall back on when and if the beer or cider they habitually carried ran out or became spoiled (not to be confused with the Georgian navy's rum ration). Sailors who had acquired a taste for spirits at sea wanted hard liquor ashore as well, a demand that soon spread to landlubbers; and, according to critics, shops and beer houses sold liquor 'so fierce and heady' that a pint 'will make half a score of men and women drunk'.

THE LONDON DISTILLER'S COMPANY

It was (ostensibly, at least) in response to the indiscriminate and unregulated spread of distilling that the London Distiller's Company was formed to control the industry within a 21-mile radius of the city. The movers behind the new livery company – sixty-ninth in order of precedence – were two fairly minor courtiers: Sir William Brouncker, who had virtually beggared himself buying a viscountcy, and the queen's physician, Thomas Cademan, a recusant Roman Catholic. The two were already in business together as distillers in St James's; and to overcome opposition from the Apothecaries' Company, they sought the advocacy of the king's own physician Sir Theodore de Mayerne, a Huguenot refugee who had attended Henry IV of France until the king's assassination in 1610 and had then joined the court of James I in London. First and foremost a chemist, he had assisted at the secession of the apothecaries from the grocers to form their own livery company in 1617. Once again his lobbying was successful, and the London Company of Distillers (never to be confused with the twentieth-century Distillers Company Ltd) received its charter as the Worshipful Company of Distillers from Charles I in August 1638 with Cademan as Master.

The Company was, on the face of it, intended to regulate and prevent abuses and protect the public, declaring in its charter: 'that no Afterworts or Wash (made by Brewers, etc.) called Blew John, nor musty unsavoury or unwholesome tilts, or dregs of beer or ale; nor unwholesome or adulterated wines, or Lees of Wines, nor unwholesome sugar-waters; musty unsavoury or unwholesome returned beer or ale; nor rotten corrupt or unsavoury fruits, druggs, spices, herbs, seeds; nor any other ill-conditioned materials of what kind soever, shall henceforth be distilled, extracted or drawn into small spirits, or low wines, or be any other ways used, directly or indirectly, by any of the Members of this Company, or their successors at any time hereafter forever.' Many of these practices were and remain industry commonplaces – and some had even been recommended by Gessner and his English translators. As for 'unwholesome wines', the thin, acidic whites that the Dutch had selected as the feedstock for their French brandy were pretty well undrinkable in their virgin state. Of course, it was all a racket: the founders charged for membership, then wrote a charter nobody could obey, and fined members when they couldn't. The Stuarts were perhaps the most overtly corrupt dynasty in British history, and this scam was one of many. But it does tell us that malt liquor was now commonly used in distillation, and English malt brandy was no different from the quasi-medicinal spirits commonly produced in the rest of northern Europe.

THE PURITANS' DILEMMA

The influence of the B-list courtiers behind the London Company of Distillers naturally waned with the outbreak of civil war in 1642. London, still at this time the principal seat of English distilling, was securely in the hands of Parliament from the moment the war started until the Restoration nearly 18 years later; and you might expect that a government of Puritans would zealously and rigorously purge it of frivolities such as distilled spirits, just as it purged it of maypoles and Christmas. But it didn't, and for two main reasons. One was that spirit beverages still existed side by side with spirit-based medicines and were in many cases produced by the very same enterprises, so that you couldn't harm one without harming the other. Another was that while the puritan ethos may have dominated politically, Puritans themselves were a minority and their culture was not universally shared even within the loose and fractious grouping of interests that comprised the Government. Nor were the Puritans a bunch of mirthless killjoys per se. The Lutheran strand in English Protestantism, as opposed to the Calvinist strand in the kirk, valued hard work, enterprise, ingenuity and initiative to the point where worldly success could be taken as a mark of Divine favour. If a brewer or an apothecary were to increase his wealth and social standing by diversifying into distilling, then provided he could contrive to appear godly he would find no enemies in the ruling coalition. What held distilling back was the state of the wartime economy: one of Parliament's first acts after hostilities began was to impose a near-universal purchase tax, the Excise (from the Dutch *accijns*), which was so onerous that it provoked a serious riot in 1647 when the butchers of Smithfield resisted the officers sent to collect it. But Excise was an exigency of war, quickly taken up by both the Royalist and Scottish Parliaments and intended as a temporary measure, not a punitive one; for while the Puritans and their fellow travellers sought to suppress any public junketings they considered ungodly, they could hardly suppress alcohol itself when beer was food for the worker, wine the reward for the diligent, and 'strong waters' the medicine for both.

'MIXT & CONFUS'D TRASH'

In the meantime, drinking spirits had been getting more popular with the English working classes, not so much in the countryside as in the burgeoning towns and cities. In the seventeenth and eighteenth centuries a still was part of the standard kitchen equipment in country houses of any note and in the grand coaching inns that aped them, and huge collections of spirit-based recipes not just for beverage but also for medicines and cosmetics were commonplace. But they were for the gentry. Good Queen Bess's peasantry stuck mainly to beer and cider, which were plentiful, cheap and available on demand.

In the towns and cities, though, apothecaries soon found it more profitable not to produce precious medicines to be prescribed by the dram, but to churn out bulk quantities of cheap and cheerful spirit which they watered down, sweetened, compounded with fruit and herbs, and turned over as quickly as possible. In the seventeenth century the most popular spirit with Londoners was aniseed-flavoured, perhaps imitating the raki, ouzo and pastis familiar to seafarers, until it was supplanted in the 1690s by gin. These spirits were mostly distilled from scratch and retailed in the 'strong-water shops' of which Daniel Defoe, born in 1660 and writing many years later, records:

'These were a sort of petty Distillers, who made up those compound Waters from such mixt and confus'd Trash, as they could get to work from, such as damag'd and eager, or sour Wines; Wines that had taken Salt Water in at Sea; Lees and Bottoms; also damag'd Sugars, and Melasses, Grounds of Syder, and innumerable other such like. For till then there was very little Distilling known in England, but for physical Uses. The Spirits they drew were foul, and gross; but they mixt them up with such Additions as they could get, to make them palatable, and so gave them in general, the Name of Cordial Waters. And thus the strong-Water-Shops usually made a vast Show of Glasses, labell'd and written on, like the Gallypot Latin of the Apothecarys, with innumerable hard Names to set them off.

As for what the poor people favoured, Defoe tells us:

'Aqua Vitae and Anniseed Water, were the Captains or Leaders; and the strong Inclinations of the People ran all into those two: And in a little while the latter prevail'd over the former too; and as Anniseed Water was the only Liquor for some Years, the Quantity that was drunk of it, was prodigious great: In a word, it was the Geneva of those Times, it was not only sold in the Chandlers Shops, and in the Barbers Shops, as above; and perhaps in Bulks and Stalls too.

ILLICIT STILLS

Eventually the heavily medicated *usquebaugh* died out, supplanted in eighteenth-century medicine by tinctures and linctuses in which the even more efficacious newcomer, opium, largely usurped the role of malt spirit; the only known living descendant of those older concoctions, reinvented as a liqueur, is Drambuie.

But if the small tenant farmers of Scotland – Lowlands as well as Highlands – and Ireland could handcraft in their primitive stills a spirit that became one of the world's gastronomic superstars, why could not the English? Well, it all boils down to the social and geographical structure of English rural organisation. The residents of communities generally large enough to host specialist craftsmen such as blacksmiths, builders, carpenters, bakers and brewers had narrower but more advanced skill sets than the wider ranging but more general capabilities of their Gaelic cousins. Except in its most basic sense – such as being able to rehang a gate or re-roof a barn – they were not jacks of all trade. They made their living by sticking to a specialism: thatchers were not blacksmiths, blacksmiths were not thatchers, and none of them were distillers. Furthermore, as either employees or at best tenants in an increasingly oppressive and unequal economy they had little spare time and even less spare cash. The poet John Clare grew up in a Northamptonshire cottage with enough room for the family and a garden with an apple tree whose produce, his father said, paid the rent. The landlord then arbitrarily divided the cottage and its garden into four tenements, moved three more families in, and reduced them all to penury (and Clare himself to madness).

Most farmworkers had neither the money nor the time even for brewing. The radical politician and journalist William Cobbett in *Cottage Economy* (1821) bemoaned the rise of tea-drinking and tried to persuade country dwellers to brew their own beer, as he supposed they had habitually done in days of yore (they hadn't). He lambasted tea as weak, enervating stuff, the bane of the labourer; but the people knew better than him, for tea was ideally suited to their requirements. When it was still taxed it wasn't cheap and was really only affordable thanks to industrial-scale adulteration; but you only used as much as you needed and, with the boiling water coming from the kettle on the kitchen range, it required no extra firing (which was expensive to buy and hard to gather when the landowner also owned the woods), and carried no substantial risk of spillage or spoilage.

But even had one of the more enterprising and talented sons of toil been tempted to fit a neck and wormtub to the family wash copper, it would have proved hard going. The village distiller would have found it daunting and possibly fatal to compete with those other purveyors of duty-free luxuries to the squirearchy, the smuggling gangs. To read the Norfolk diarist Parson Woodforde's anxiety as to future supplies of brandy and other essentials (including tea) when John Buck, blacksmith and smuggler of the parish, was arrested (only a temporary interruption, fortunately) one might think that these people were harmless: quaint figures in a quaint landscape. They weren't. Like smugglers everywhere, they'd turn on you in an instant if you posed any threat and might, like the notorious Hawkhurst Gang in Sussex, be both torturers and murderers.

Even without the dangers of competing with people who had a way of dealing with competition, the dingly dells of Georgian England were also lethal to anyone engaged in clandestine nocturnal activities. Picturesque the woods and meadows may have been in sunlight or snow, but after dark they became free-fire zones patrolled by homicidal gamekeepers whose arsenals of spring-guns and mantraps, bloodhounds and mastiffs, and blunderbusses on permanent half-cock were mainly intended for poachers but would just as easily kill a moonshiner tending his still. As a result, hill and dale were devoid of moonshiners.

Well, not entirely. A remarkable piece of field research conducted for the Northumberland National Park Authority has revealed the existence of a number of illicit stills and shebeens, known locally as whisky houses, along a busy and important drove-road from Scotland southward through Coquetdale in the eighteenth and nineteenth centuries. The shebeens not only sheltered, fed and watered (!) the drovers themselves but were also social focuses for the local sheep-men. These prosperous Borderers seem to have been as much Scottish as English, being not only whisky-drinkers but Presbyterians to boot; and the trade was so brazenly conducted that as the railway network spread the whisky-house proprietors supplemented locally made mountain dew with supplies of genuine Scotch imported through Newcastle. The very same trains killed the whole business in the end, though: once the cattle took to the rail Coquetdale all but died, and all that is left of its little whisky industry are sad heaps of overgrown masonry.

The same could be said of the village of Haslingden Grane in the upper Ogden valley near Rossendale, Lancashire. It too is now represented by no more than a few forlorn huddles of dressed stone marking the foundations of farmsteads, cottages and spinning sheds made less and less viable by the creation of reservoirs to serve mill towns like Bolton and Blackburn and by the quarrying of the stone required to build them. The last residents departed in 1920, but less than a century before that Haslingden Grane had been a ragged row of humble homes (including a pub, the Holden Arms, which is still there today) stretched out along the lane over the moors, housing some 600 souls at its peak – and an unknown number of unlicensed whisky stills.

The Whisky Spinners of Haslingden Grane have long been well-known figures in local lore and, indeed, in well-documented local history; but they have only recently come to much wider prominence thanks to foodsofengland.co.uk and its founder, the guerrilla food historian Glynn Hughes who has collected data on all sorts of English fare from offal to toffee, not forgetting the forgotten English pasta of the fourteenth century.

Moonshining here flourished from the 1830s to at least the 1860s; from 1834–1848 the village even had a resident revenue officer of its own. It is not known – or if it is, it is only known to a few – what event or whose inspiration ignited the moonshine in Grane, but it is possible to enumerate the conditions that made it feasible. The village had had a dominant family in the sixteenth and seventeenth centuries, the Hartleys, but no resident squire after that to maintain discipline (there were chapels, but they don't seem to have put much of a brake on the business). The village was remote but not so remote that the spirit-loving millhands of Haslingden itself, Rawtenstall and Rossendale were out of reach. There was enough movement on the roads to camouflage the illegal traffic, and the bales of homespun carried by pack pony from the cottagers' handlooms to the urban woollen mills covered their secret loads of three- or four-gallon tin canisters of spirit well enough to survive cursory inspection. The region's distance from the West Coast ports meant there was little contraband rum to be had, while its distance from the East Coast ports made contraband brandy and Dutch gin equally scarce. A population dependent equally on agricultural and light-industrial trades possessed all the skills necessary for both the cultivation of barley – the true staff of life in the hills, where most people never or seldom tasted wheaten bread – and the construction, operation and maintenance of small pot stills which could easily be broken down into their innocent components in the unlikely event of a revenue officer chancing by. The times were right, too: the decades that followed the Napoleonic Wars were just as poverty-stricken, brutal,

Haslingden Grane looking east across the reservoirs.

oppressed and generally desperate for workers in both town and country in England as in blighted Ireland and the Scottish Highlands of the Clearances. The chance for small cottagers to transform a few bits of barley into liquid gold was too great an opportunity to pass up; and one wonders how much time each batch spent in oak, and how much of the deficiency was made up by the addition of caramel or even tar. But the proof of the pudding was in the eating, or rather the drinking: the stuff sold. Nor was it only the handloom weavers, the slow death of whose trade ensured an equally slow death for many of them, the owners of the village's three powered looms were just as avid and rather more prolific moonshiners. The cellars of their derelict factories have yielded up the impressive remnants of industrial-scale stills; and one of the whisky spinners, Robert Morris, was in 1849 fined £230 plus costs for evading £700 in duty in the course of a year – absolutely staggering sums. The life-changing potential of illicit distilling in the Ogden valley was so great that we can only wonder how many similar locations hosted the same industry.

There was another fairly major episode of moonshining in England that needs to be accounted for. Industrial expansion sucked tens of thousands of immigrants into the ready-made slums of cities such as Liverpool, Manchester, Birmingham and the West Riding. Many of these incomers were English peasant families driven off the land by enclosures, but just as many others were displaced Irish and Scottish farmworkers who brought with them both a thirst for whisky and the skills to quench it. In 1831 it was estimated that there were 100 illegal stills being operated by Irishmen in Manchester alone, and there were more, too, in the less populous Lancashire mill-towns such as Blackburn and Bolton, which at one time had 21. Illicit distilling seems to have been confined to the north and north-west of England partly because these regions were not so well supplied by the smuggling gangs of the South and East coasts, as we have seen; but partly, also, because of their concentrations of immigrant labour.

More efficient policing, a paramilitary Customs service blooded and battle-hardened in the unrelenting war against the smuggling gangs, sensible duty reforms, and competition from the reasonably priced and consistent blended and bottled Scotch whiskies introduced in the 1860s killed it off; but if a thorough search of the English countryside reveals almost no trace of whisky distilling, where did all those hundreds of thousands of gallons of the stuff we noted earlier come from? Well, mostly from the gin-distilling industry, you won't be surprised to learn, and specifically from three seaward-facing distilleries in England's largest West Coast port cities, Bristol and Liverpool.

EARLY ENGLISH DISTILLERIES

In 1887 Harper's Wine & Spirit Gazette published a ground-breaking book, *The Whisky Distilleries of the United Kingdom*, by one of its regular contributors, Alfred Barnard. Barnard and some companions had visited 157 whisky distilleries in Scotland and Ireland and four in England during 1885–6, and Barnard wrote them up from an engineer's viewpoint. Every tube, tub and vat were described in detail but the history, ownership and other vital statistics of each plant was only sketchily reported, if at all, and of tasting notes – in the case of the English four, at least – are there none. Still, these are the best and most detailed records we possess from this or indeed any other period, so we might as well make the most of them.

Three of the four started life as all-purpose distillers making plain spirit either as industrial alcohol or for sale to rectifiers as the base for their gin. They branched out into supplying the whisky industry with grain spirit in the 1860s when the Scottish bottler Andrew Usher started making consistent blends of grain and malt spirits for bottling

– a tremendous novelty then – triggering a huge demand for grain spirit that could only be met by the big industrial concerns whose main customers had hitherto been gin rectifiers.

The oldest was the Bristol distillery in what was then Cheese Lane, an industrial area which was home to a clay-pipe maker, among other industries, but was bombed out in December 1940 and has since been completely redeveloped. The distillery's origins supposedly lay in the seventeenth century, but almost nothing is known about its early days. By the time of Barnard's tour of inspection it had been in the hands of a family named Board for three generations and seems to have been principally a spirit distillery producing more than 600,000 gallons of plain maize-based spirit intended for rectifying, denaturing and blending. The Mr Board who showed Barnard round boasted that the firm had been making pure malt (although of poor reputation, according to a lone notice, with a distinct tang of creosote probably masking its youth) as long ago as the reign of George III; however, by Barnard's visit its output was mainly exported directly to blenders in Ireland and Scotland.

The two Liverpool distilleries, Vauxhall and Bank Hall, were founded in 1781 and 1795 respectively by the same family of local magnates, the Prestons. They were both big grain distilleries – annual output of 2,000,000 and 1,500,000 proof gallons respectively – which had diversified, like the Bristol distillery, into grain whisky production in the 1860s to satisfy demand for blending spirits in Scotland and Ireland. Both, Barnard reported almost droolingly, were lavishly equipped with the most modern plant available. Vauxhall, which the Preston family sold to Archibald Walker & Co of the Adelphi Distillery, Glasgow, in 1857, may have been a delayed-action victim of the Pattison Brothers collapse of 1898, Pattison Brothers was a firm of blenders and bottlers in Leith which borrowed and borrowed and borrowed to buy far more fillings than it could ever sell and which duly foundered, leaving dozens of unpaid suppliers drowning in its wake. The Distillers Company, a consortium of the biggest grain distillers, snapped up many struggling malt distillers to secure its supplies, restored some order to the industry and in 1908 bought Vauxhall as well. The story is told in the proceedings of the *Royal Commission on Whiskey & Other Potable Spirits*, published in February 1909 in which the word whisky is spelled whiskey throughout.

Bank Hall, meanwhile, seems to have struggled along, still under family ownership, until the 1920s. It cannot have been making gin during World War I when barley supplies were severely restricted; but Barnard notes that in 1886 it was a considerable producer of

Bank Hall Distillery, Sandhills, Liverpool.

PROPRIETORS, R. W. PRESTON & CO., LIMITED.

THE next day, as arranged the previous evening, our party of three walked from the hotel to St. George's Hall, one of the lions of Liverpool. It is a noble building, with a magnificent central hall, round which are ranged the law courts and municipal offices. After this we adjourned to the Walker Gallery, the munificent gift of a generous citizen, which contains priceless treasures of art, which we regretted that we had not time to study. We then adjourned to the Athenæum, as one of our friends wished to unearth some information respecting the derivation of the name of Liverpool. The Athenæum, which consists of a library and reading-rooms, was opened in 1799, and was the first of its kind in the country, and gave rise to those of London, Manchester, and Bristol. The origin of the name of Liverpool is very obscure; some say it is derived from a species of liver-wort found on the sea shore—others, with more probability, ascribe it to the Welsh words Lle'r-pwll, signifying "the place on the pool." The pool on the borders of which the original town stood occupied the site of the Custom House. Baxter supposes this to have been the port of the *Sestantii*, mentioned by Ptolemy, but this is doubtful, as it is generally supposed that the town did not even exist at the time of the Conquest. In the beginning of the sixteenth century, Leland gives this description of it: "Lyverpoole, a paved towne hath but a chapel, Walton at 4 miles off, not far from the se is paroche chirch"; and in 1571 the place is mentioned in a petition to Queen Elizabeth as "her majesty's poor decayed town of Liverpool." In this reign, however, a mole was formed to lay up the vessels in during the winter, and a quay for shipping. It was in the reign of William III. that Liverpool was made into a distinct parish from Walton-on-the-Hill, and since that time the town has grown into a great city, and the greatest port in the British Empire.

On leaving the Athenæum, we drove to the Bank Hall Establishment, distant from the hotel three miles. It is a modern work, built of stone, with a frontage to the main road of 450 feet, and covers five acres of ground. Owing to the close proximity of the public grain warehouses, it is not necessary to keep a large stock on the premises; nevertheless, the Company have devoted several floors of one of their large buildings to that purpose. The grain from the public warehouses is delivered by waggons to the Distillery, and raised to the various floors of the Corn Lofts and Mill buildings by a steam hoist.

On presenting our credentials, we were conducted, by one of the junior partners, over the establishment, and commenced our inspection at the Mill

The Bankhall Distillery entry taken from The Whisky Distilleries of the United Kingdom by Alfred Barnard and first published in 1887.

denatured (i.e. contaminated with methanol and other poisons) industrial spirit as well as plain spirit, grain whisky and malt whisky; perhaps it supplied the munitions and motor-fuel industries during the war. It might well have soldiered on in this fashion for quite some while afterwards; however, it seems to have given up the ghost during the Depression.

Which brings me to the fourth of Barnard's list of English whisky distilleries and perhaps, apart from those humble Coquetdale bothies and Lancashire basements, the only one in England's entire history (until now, of course) that could fairly be described as principally a whisky distillery at all: East London's own, its very own, Lea Valley.

Although it was a commercial flop, London's only (until now, of course) whisky distillery has become celebrated for being pressed into service to publicise the launch of Battersea's London Distillery Company (LDC) in 2011, which played on the fact that here was London's first whisky distillery for more than a century. No reporter or reviewer could mention the LDC without repeating the line thereafter, so that it became the only thing anybody knew about either enterprise. It was as if Lea Valley had been subsumed into LDC's very soul; sadly, in a way it had, for their stories are similar.

Described by Barnard as the only malt distillery in England – although the others made malt as well as grain spirit, and Lea Valley made grain as well as malt – it was incorporated in 1882 and located on Warton Road, Stratford, on a tributary of the River Lea very close to the enormous Three Mills gin distillery. All trace of it finally disappeared under the Olympic Park, but Barnard described it and its equipment in almost lustful detail, giving an impression of a very spacious state-of-the-art facility. 'It was certainly a bold experiment to make a trial in the very heart of the kingdom, so far away from the hills and mountain streams,' he wrote after his tour, only four years after it had opened. 'The proprietors find, by experience, that they did wisely, and that demand for their whisky has led to the erection of other buildings as well as the extension of those existing.' The company, he added, had also gone in for the production of grain whisky.

Such boldness was hardly congruous with the balance sheet. A good rummage in the National Archives at Kew by Brian Strong of London Industrial Archaeology has revealed that the launch offer of 5000 shares at £20 had only attracted 961 subscribers, raising a mere £19,000. In 1894 the company was wound up and relaunched with an offer of 2500 shares at £10, but again with few takers. Ten years later, following the death of some of the founders and the departure of others and, of course, in the wake of the cataclysmic Pattison

Brothers collapse, the distillery was closed and wound up for good. Some researchers believe it was offered to Distillers Company Ltd (DCL), but if so DCL was not interested. Little is known of what happened next, but by 1910 the buildings had been expunged from the Ordnance Survey map.

BATTERSEA, BERMONDSEY, BUST

The London Distillery Company, incorporated in 2011 and dissolved in January 2022, had an even shorter but even stormier life than Lea Valley. Founded like Lea Valley by two ambitious entrepreneurs, it too was chronically undercapitalised and its early reputation for innovation and quality – organic rye whisky, malt made from an obsolete ale barley, Plumage Archer, grown on King Charles's Highgrove Estate, collaborations with Kew Gardens and Fortnum & Mason – did nothing to ease its underfunding, which was compounded by sheer bad luck. Its original home in the cold room of a Victorian dairy in Battersea, was acquired for redevelopment and it took eight months to find a new site in a railway arch in Bermondsey's Beer Mile and get it appropriately licensed. The partners went their separate ways after a row with HMRC; a bold plan to move to Battersea Power Station had to be axed; and in 2020 the company went into administration. Whisky production ceased, and its gin brands were bought by the British Honey Company just as Covid was making its appearance. In 2022 the company was finally wound up and the site was acquired by Halewood Vintners as a new and rather chic home for its Whitley Neill family of deluxe gins.

A WALK ON THE WELSH SIDE

Sons and daughters of Cymru will have observed, no doubt with displeasure, that the land of their fathers has entirely escaped notice in the opening section of this book. That this is a book about English whisky is no excuse for such outrageous neglect: we have virtually wallowed in Scotch, and Irish has had its mention too. So why no drop of Welsh?

Well, not because there was no tradition of distilling in Wales. The very cradle of British monasticism cannot have been without its infirmarers tending their retorts and dispensing their potions and lotions. If they were anything like other infirmarers, then once they had been pensioned off and cast adrift following the Dissolution of the Monasteries in the 1530s they will have carried their skills with them to the market-place and thence to the world. But as in England, so in Wales. Unlike Scotland and Ireland, no tradition of home distilling seems to have emerged here; or if it did, the spirit thus produced seems to have escaped the oaken chrysalis that elsewhere transformed the caterpillar usquebaugh into the butterfly whisky.

But only 'seems'. Records are sketchy and what little we know of the history of distilling in Wales suggests that drinking spirits never gained much of a foothold. There are suggestions that two well-known names in early American whiskey-making, Jack Daniels and Evan Williams, came from families of distillers back in Wales, but there is not nearly enough evidence to take these stories seriously. It is, of course, entirely possible, not to say inevitable, that many of the Welsh emigrants to North America in the eighteenth and nineteenth centuries were indeed distillers, as were so many Scottish and Irish; but on balance they were more likely to have been apothecaries and horse-doctors rather than nascent whiskey barons.

One reason for supposing so is that the Chapel, that ambient consensus of 101 Nonconformist denominations, was a rising power across Wales from the 1730s on; and being inspired by Calvin rather than Wesley the ministers of the country's constellation of chapels were sternly authoritarian and firmly against innocent pleasures such as drink. Rural immigrants to the industrial population centres of South Wales from the 1790s brought their religious *hywl* with them, so spirit-drinking was denied its customary popularity in semi-derelict slum court and damp rabbit-hutch terrace. Distillers may have made elixirs and cordials – particularly decongestants in the mining districts, one imagines – by the gallon, and rum was popular on the cosmopolitan quaysides of Cardiff and Swansea; but of whisky we hear very little.

There was, in 1889, a solitary attempt to establish a large commercial distillery in north Wales at Frongoch near Bala in Merionethshire. Its output, though, was not intended to supply Welsh throats so much as the growing Scottish and Irish fillings markets. But Merionethshire was firmly in the north-west Welsh heartland of Calvinism, and such a depravity as a distillery was *not* what pious people wanted to see on their way to chapel on a Sunday morning. Such was the ferocity of the recriminations bellowed from the region's pulpits that the Welsh Whisky Company took to accepting its various trade deliveries at night. The distillery lasted only until 1900, but it was not the contumely of the godly that doomed it. According to the leading whisky writer Charles McLean, it was the cheap half-seasoned oak it used. The site (long gone now: it was a prison camp in World War I and was demolished in the 1920s) was acknowledged to be ideal in every respect, yet the whisky itself was mysteriously vile.

If that were the whole tale of Welsh whisky, then its absence from a book about English whisky could be forgiven, just about. And yet the pathway of today's English whisky runs not directly from Scotland, as might be imagined: it first makes a great winding detour through the unmarked and untraceable ruins of Frongoch, via the long-defunct brewhouse behind the Camden Arms away to the south in Brecon, and finally to a brand-new distillery on the rim of the Brecon Beacons.

The Camden Arms' landlord Dafydd Gittins not only pulled pints but also dabbled in mead, supplying the mock-medieval banquets that, like chicken in a basket and weak keg beers, were the gastronomical highlights of the times. One fateful day in or about 1970, or so Dafydd told the *Chicago Tribune* during a US promotional tour, he had come across a Frongoch bottle in the banqueting hall he was delivering to and started nosing about in the hope of finding out more about it. In Bala Library he discovered an old recipe for a pretty standard medicinal compound of spirit steeped in a nosegay of curative and prophylactical weeds. But instead of thinking immediately of 'Lily the Pink' (then in the charts) and cooking up an elixir most efficacious in every case, his romantic imagination provided him with the idea that there had once been a genuine traditional Welsh whisky.

In a scene familiar to any new-wave gin maker, Dafydd then spent years locked in the pub's old brewhouse trying out different combinations of botanicals to be steeped in fillings imported from Scotland. In 1974 he found a suitable grist of salad leaves (local, of course) and was soon marketing Prince of Wales and Swyn o Mor ('gentle sea breeze') as very pleasant and characterful Welsh blends, diluted to bottle strength with pure Brecon spring water. The marketing itself was as questionable as the blends. He claimed to have come across in his research an account of the monks of Bardsey Island, nearly 75 years before the abbey there was founded, distilling liquor some 400 years before wine was first distilled in Persia more than 3000 miles away. The story is a complete invention, then, and an absurd one at that. But in its 50-odd years it has become the accepted orthodoxy and churned out endlessly.

It also seems that Dafydd invented the cod-Welsh word *chwisgi* to describe his unWelsh whisky. To be fair, it may have been a real word: the Welsh are very proficient at transliterating English where their own language is lacking, as in *telefon* and *ambwlans*. But to do him justice, he may have been impatient and oppositional, and he may have indulged in, to be charitable, tongue-in-cheek marketing;

but his purpose was serious. The US export drive alone is evidence of that, but there's more. He wanted to design a new still, faster, cheaper and more energy-efficient than the traditional copper pot. To this end he commissioned two University of Surrey lecturers, David Faraday and Ron Schultz, to design one and got a European grant to have it fabricated at McMillans of Prestonpans. The secret of the Faraday still, which is essentially a rectifying column mounted on a big, 2500-litre pot where the neck and lyne arm ought to be and looking not unlike a fairly standard gin still, lies inside the column. This contains an array of condensation plates whose configuration can be altered by the use of pumps to remove only the required fractions. It tends to work rather like a gin still as well as looking like one: it produces a clean, light spirit which has been accused of blandness; but when it was commissioned lighter spirits were a bit of a pot of gold as far as the industry was concerned; and had the Faraday still been turned on it would have produced something contemporary, on trend and really quite exciting.

But it was not to be. The still had been set up and ready to be fired up since 1993 when the Scotch Whisky Association (SWA) pounced and had Dafydd prosecuted under European law for passing off – so there you go: there's the EC (as it was then) for you, giving with one hand and taking away with the other. The partners who bought him out fared even worse, attracting the ire of Her Majesty's Customs & Excise – a far more fearsome beast than the SWA and the EC – who jailed them for filling in some forms wrong. And so for *chwisgi Cymraeg*, the game was up.

But in 1997 the revolutionary still, its associated bottling line and sundry bits and pieces were bought out of liquidation for £75,000 by local businessmen, headed by Welsh Development Agency chief economist Brian Morgan, who had perfectly viable plans for relaunching the whole business. They started by moving it from Brecon to a newly built site at Penderyn, on the far side of the Beacons, and then – since none of them had ever distilled a drop themselves – engaged the services of one of Scotland's finest distilling consultants, the late but legendary Dr Jim Swan who was also deeply involved in the early days of two important English distilleries (see page 48). Dr Swan's rectifications included finishing the rather light whisky in Madeira and oloroso casks, contracting out the brewing of the wash to Brain's of Cardiff, and sorting out the still's teething troubles. Spirit finally started dripping into the receiver in 2000, but even then the new era got off to a poor start. The normal bridging tactics – white spirit production and cask sales – didn't deliver the necessaries, and

The late Dr Jim Swan, distilling consultant to Penderyn distillery.

Mr Morgan had to raise £1,000,000 to keep the venture afloat. This entailed bringing in a new CEO, Stephen Davies, and output grew steadily, necessitating the installation of a second Faraday still as well as two conventional pots to fatten the whisky up a bit (and more recently the opening of two more distilleries at Swansea and Llandudno). A young bottling was thus possible in 2004, and, well... we're getting too Welsh, so it's time to head back up the A465, the A466 and the A40 to Monmouth and good old England.

Before we cross the border, though, Welsh traditionalists will point you to line 7 of Taliesin's 'Can y Medd' or 'Song of Mead', number XIX in the Llyfr Taliesin, which dates to about 550 and in English goes thus: 'Mead distilled sparkling, its praise is everywhere', as proof that there was distillation in early medieval Wales. Well, there wasn't. Modern scholars reckon that only the first XII poems are genuine, and the manuscript is a sixteenth-century copy of a thirteenth-century poem. By the thirteenth century distilling was a pharmaceutical commonplace; and anyway, however sparkling a drink is when it goes into the still, by the time it drips out again it's as flat as a pancake.

CHAPTER TWO

HEROES & VILLAINS

HOW THE RENAISSANCE BEGAN

'My father's sole ambition was to produce the very finest single malt whisky. This is still the only goal of The English Distillery.'

ANDREW NELSTROP

Inside the warehouse at St George's Distillery, now known as The English Distillery.

Although Dafydd Gittins has always been painted as a bit fly, his record shows him to have been a determined and studious man nursing a very serious ambition. And if only he had been a little more straightforward in presenting himself and his mission the whole craft distilling revival might have been kicked off in Brecon in the late 1970s or early '80s. But he wasn't, and it didn't, and instead the world had to wait a few years for the arrival of two men who were equally ambitious.

TWO CIDER GIANTS TURNED DISTILLERS AND HEROES

It was the newly retired chairman of HP Bulmer, the (then) Hereford-based cidermaker, who was responsible for reintroducing the art of (legal) distillation south of the border. Bertram Bulmer (d. 1993) had the confidence that comes with being a scion of a dynamic and powerful family and with having been a director of the world's biggest cidermaker for more than half a century – since the age of 22, in fact.

A major retirement project of his was the foundation of the Hereford Cider Museum in the building in Ryelands Street where pomagne had once been made by the méthode champenoise. To help fund the museum, which opened in 1981, it was decided to use an old pot still acquired from Normandy to make cider and perry brandy under the King Offa label. A licence to distill was granted by HM Customs & Excise, rather to the surprise of HM Customs & Excise, in 1984; and in 1987 the first fruits went on sale. The first bottle was given to Queen Elizabeth II while the second went to the then Prince of Wales, both of whom had donated oak from their estates to be turned into barrels.

At this point the French objected to the use of the name 'cider brandy' on the grounds that the word brandy could only be used to denote a distillate of wine – even though there is no such word, nor even an equivalent, in French. It came as news to companies that had been calling their fruit macerations 'cherry brandy' and 'apricot brandy' for generations, and Bulmer simply ignored an instruction to rename his product 'cider spirit'. British officialdom found itself, much to its surprise, going in to bat for King Offa, and the French objection was headed off. This did not stop distillers from Spain, Scotland and Italy raising the same objection against Julian Temperley of Burrow

Hill Cider, who in 1987 had started making cider brandy on another ancient French still in partnership with Charles Clive-Ponsonby-Fane of Brympton D'Evercy Hall near Yeovil. It took four years of legal wrangling to overcome the objections this time, perhaps because Temperley wasn't quite as well-connected as Bertram Bulmer.

In 1989 Temperley moved out of Brympton D'Evercy and set up the Somerset Cider Brandy Company at Thorney nearby, using two small Norman continuous stills, originally alembics ambulants that went from farm to farm distilling fresh-made cider, dubbed Josephine and Fifi. Somerset Royal Cider Brandy and its various extensions – different ages and bottlings, eaux de vie, aperitifs and liqueurs – provoked intense interest in the food and drink media and inspired a great many other cidermakers too. Temperley went on to distil cider for Bridge Farm and Yarde Farm of Stoke Gabriel, Devon, and for the monks of Ampleforth Abbey in North Yorkshire. Healey's Cornish Cyder at Penhallow used a small Scottish pot still to make its cider brandy; while the Herefordshire potato grower William Chase turned both his distilled cider and his potato crop, once used for making Tyrrells Crisps, not into brandy but into William's Gin and Naked Vodka.

When the cider giants applied for their licences to distil, Customs & Excise was not only unsure of what drawers the requisite forms were kept in, nobody even knew what one looked like. In spite of European regulations, though, in spite of HM Customs & Excise, in spite of dungeon, fire and sword, Bertram Bulmer and Julian Temperley became the inspirations behind the whole new wave of craft distilling, and the heroes to whom we owe a great debt of gustatory gratitude.

But they are far from being the only heroes. Movements like microbrewing, English winemaking and artisanal distilling depend on heroes – all too often, alas, the pioneers over whose bodies the settlers step. Let's meet a few.

A SELECTION OF HEROES

A key component of extreme heroism is red rage; another is innumeracy. And as red rage in the face of uncounted and perhaps uncountable odds generally disqualifies you from being cool, calm and collected, then a third component of heroism is all too often failure and death, which is no good to anybody really. If you're going to storm a bunker come what may, do remember to bring some hand grenades with you. Dafydd Gittins was one of those heroes. He had his faults, true, of which the worst was that he failed. He was the kind of hero you tend to find dead in ditches.

His successors have been no less heroic in their way: they, too, undertook daunting endeavours with a fine disregard for the risk, but at least they sharpened their bayonets before charging. They come, unlike the microbrewing pioneers before them who tended to have backgrounds in mainstream brewing, from all walks of life, a variety the heroes saluted herewith have been selected to represent.

JAMES NELSTROP: THE FOUNDER OF THE FEAST

James Nelstrop was born into a farming family in Lincolnshire and carved out a career as a widely respected international agricultural entrepreneur. He became well-known in the industry for his work on reclaiming poor and depleted land and improving agricultural techniques in Australia and Russia. After starting his farming career in Lincolnshire he emigrated with his young family to Australia before returning to farm in Norfolk in 1977, where he had bought an arable farm at Roudham in Norfolk. Here he introduced centre-pivot irrigation to transform big stretches of Breckland's sandy and infertile soil into productive arable land and grew the barley that was to dominate his later life. For it was here at Roudham that he was later to build St George's Distillery (recently renamed The English Distillery), complete with its Doig-style pagoda.

While farming at Roudham he set up Nuffield Russia Trust, a charity which was to improve farming techniques in Russia by building an agricultural college and model farm. He also set up Britain's first whole farm Countryside Stewardship scheme, reviving an exhausted vegetable farm in the fens near Lakenheath as an organic sheep and cattle farm and a haven for wildlife, especially birds.

His family soon realised that despite turning 60 James had no intention of retiring but would find a different outlet for his energy, albeit something still tied into farming. He and his son Andrew – also a farmer, and an entrepreneur in the construction industry as well – decided to pursue a subject close to his heart: whisky distilling, which had died out in England 100 years previously. They had chosen the right place for it: Britain's, and indeed the world's best malting barley, is grown in Norfolk and the pure Breckland water is ideal for distilling. They considered several concepts and conducted a great deal of research in Scotland, Ireland and Wales; and in 2005 submitted their planning application, which was approved in January 2006.

Although the initial idea had been for a micro-distillery (there were already several microbreweries in the area), Customs wouldn't

Andrew Nelstrop inside the still house at The English Distillery, founded by his father James Nelstrop.

in those days consider licensing a still any smaller than 1800-litre capacity (larger than some in Scotland). So, in a field down by the River Thet, the footings were dug for a much larger distillery than they had originally envisaged and the building work began, with Andrew at the helm as main contractor.

'We were fortunate that Iain Henderson, a distiller of some note from Laphroaig, although ready to retire, was talked into coming along to help get us going,' says Andrew. 'In autumn 2006 we were able to make the first 29 barrels of English whisky and by August 2007 we opened to the public with a visitor centre, whisky shop and tours.'

Iain soon retired again, but before he did he spent 16 weeks training David Fitt, a brewer from Greene King, to take over. From 2008 David held the role of head distiller and as well as overseeing the production from washback to spirit receiver, he also watched the whisky while it was sleeping and ran the bottling line. In 2022 he handed the reins to another brewer from Greene King, Chris Waters. Since the original distillations back in 2006, thousands of casks have been filled. The distillery creates both unpeated and peated whisky, as well as having a rolling programme of cask trials, which have resulted in some wonderful small batch releases.

James died in September 2014 aged only 69, leaving Andrew to carry on and develop the trailblazing company. 'My father's sole ambition was to produce the very finest single malt whisky. This is still the only goal of The English Distillery,' says Andrew.

DAN SZOR: FINANCIER TURNED FANCIER

New Yorker and whisky aficionado Dan spent 26 years as a currency trader in Paris and London before his eureka moment on a trip to Bruichladdich in 2013. Ten years earlier he had bought a cask to lay down. He was on his annual pilgrimage to visit it and give it a hug when he mentioned to the distillery manager Jim McEwan that he'd been thinking about a distillery of his own. Jim simply told him to get on with it; and a mere 14 months later Dan was able to fire up his 500-litre Holstein gin still while his two Forsyth pot stills – a 2400-litre wash still and a 1600-litre spirit still – had only to be connected to the gas before his first batch of new make dripped from the condenser.

Luck, it must be said, had played its part in the breakneck pace of developments. Exactly the right premises in the form of a newly built house and barn, empty as the result of a planning wrangle, came on the market just five miles away from Dan's country home. The house was perfect for the laboratory, offices and shop. The pot stills from Forsyth's had been bespoke but appeared suddenly on the open market as the result of a cancellation. The boss of Warminster Maltings told Dan about a local farmer with 2000 acres of organic Odyssey barley on his hands; and then Dan, purely fortuitously, was able to buy and reopen the Malvern Mineral Water spring, once a leading national brand but which had closed three years earlier. So the barley and the water are genuinely local, and the maltings is only a county away; the Cotswolds Distillery can therefore proclaim its whisky to be as true to its terroir as any Scottish single malt.

Dan may seem an unlikely candidate to found a whisky distillery in the English countryside; but on reflection he's actually a very likely candidate indeed. Like many expats he is free of preconceptions and takes his adopted environment at face value. American culture vultures with deep pockets are a long-established stereotype, and nothing is beyond them. The export of London Bridge to Arizona is legend, but on a humbler level the ornate Georgian plaster ceilings of Croome Court, the stately home-turned-boarding school where I had my first job, had not only been removed and shipped home by

Dan Szor, founder of the Cotswolds Distillery.

some American Croesus but had been replaced by accurate-to-the-millimetre reproductions as part of the price. That was what the man wanted, and he was blind to all obstacles.

Dan, though no Croesus himself, was more than merely familiar with the ways of money but was an expert in it. He was one of those men who people with money trust to turn it into more money, and he deployed all his years of expertise in raising the humungous sums his vision demanded. How humungous? Well, he has raised £12,000,000 over the years in crowdfunding projects alone. To enquire further as to where the money came from and how much it tots up to would be impertinent, but the answers would be (a) all over and (b) lots. Not only did he cash in his own pension, but he also tapped his City contacts to invest in a Founders' Circle... at £50,000 a pop.

Dan is no culture vulture, though, or at least, not overtly. There will be no Glyndebourne Opera at Bishop's Cleeve. No, Dan is a foodie who has been able to indulge his taste for fine wines and whiskies at vineyards, distilleries and gourmet gatherings all over Europe. Here he has mingled with some of the most educated palates on the Continent and heard the word directly from the people behind the products. It was on these peregrinations that the idea of starting his own distillery crept insidiously into his head; and when he mentioned it to friends, he found they liked the idea. Not only was Dan experienced enough to grasp the scale of the project, but everything seemed to be falling into place as naturally as if destiny had got him by the scruff. In 2014, the Cotswolds Distillery was established. And yes, things did not always go to plan. There were vicissitudes, especially Covid; and a dramatic change of course early on when the original gin proved so popular that a carefully worked out schedule of expansion had to be rewritten; but the two vital attributes Dan had picked up along his life's journey – acumen and a bulging address book – always saw the good ship Cotswolds safely through the squalls. Its ducks, thanks to Dan, were well and truly in a row.

PAUL CURRIE: WHISKY ARISTOCRACY

When it came to opening a brand-new whisky distillery, Paul Currie had an advantage over all the rest: he'd done it before.

Paul was working in the oil industry with BP when he joined forces with his father and brother to start what was the first new independent malt whisky distillery in Scotland in decades. At the time Paul was working to establish BP's presence in immediate post-Soviet Poland and Russia, but he quit his job and returned to the UK to take on the role of MD, with his father Harold as chairman. Harold, then retired and in his seventies, was a well-known figure in the whisky industry after being MD with both Chivas and Pernod Ricard, so whisky was in Paul's blood. He had been surrounded by it, metaphorically at least, since early childhood; and knowing both the whisky industry and marketing he correctly foretold that in the prospering markets of the EU, the USA and the Far East there was huge potential for ultra-premium malt whiskies.

Isle of Arran was the first new independent distillery in Scotland for decades and has been credited with being the world's first new artisan distillery, of which there are now many hundreds. It was truly visionary and was a particularly difficult project to see home. As a new concept, it drew a lot of scepticism and indeed outright hostility from planners and environmentalists, who tried to scupper the project entirely. It was also a difficult build, with work being suspended to take account of the golden eagles nesting nearby. But the prospect of work and tourism won over both the community and, apparently, the golden eagles themselves, who put in a majestic if unscripted appearance at the grand opening in 1995.

Mr Currie senior retired, this time for good when Isle of Arran was sold to a group of independent investors. Paul stayed on for a while but eventually left to pursue his next dream, and he discovered it in the Lake District. In 2011, he joined forces with his co-founder, Nigel Mills, and they found and bought a stunning Victorian model dairy farm, which had been empty for 20 years. This time there was very limited opposition. Rather the opposite: the imposing dairy, built like a castle around its courtyard, was an asset crying out to be used and was perfectly designed.

The site he chose had the added advantage of location, making it a potentially huge tourist attraction. Isle of Arran had from the outset a flourishing tourist business, being a well-known holiday island, and Paul was keen to replicate this in the Lake District – but, given the number of tourists already drawn to the region, on an even larger scale. The choice of site proved a winner, and soon after its opening in 2014, The Lakes Distillery was drawing 100,000 visitors a year.

Paul also showed a canny streak in overcoming the three-year drought with no income. Instead of waiting for his new make to come of age, and alongside gin and vodka and his own-blend Scotch and other whiskies, he launched The Lakes Founder Members' Club. This was, at the time, a new concept allowing members to reserve bottlings of exclusive Lakes single malt for 10 years and attracted more than 2500 members. Just about every new distillery has since launched a similar scheme, allowing Paul to say that he came up with the instrument that underpinned the financial foundations of the entire industry.

LAURENCE CONISBEE: MILTON KEYNES NOMAD

Laurence Conisbee started making cider commercially on his girlfriend's family fruit farm in Essex in 1995 under the name Hogshead. The venture lasted as long as the relationship did, which was three years; and after the partners split up Laurence, a cartographer by trade, moved to Milton Keynes where he drifted like a virtual Marie Celeste into generic IT.

But Laurence was perpetually looking for something more fulfilling to do and in 2009 returned to cidermaking at his home, despite his garden being utterly devoid of apples. Friends whose gardens did have apple trees, however, kept him supplied; and he supplemented their donations by patrolling the leafy lanes of Milton Keynes gathering what bounty nature offered. Then a friend who worked for the city authorities arranged matters so that Laurence got permission to pick on all its parks and gardens, which included a small orchard. Almost overnight Virtual Orchard – very punny, Laurence, very punny – was a serious concern; and matters got even further out of hand in

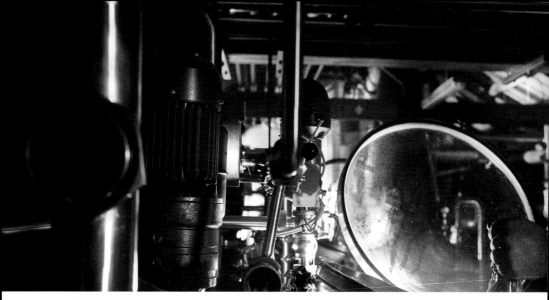

Taking a sample from a washback at The Lakes Distillery. The distillery was co-founded in 2011 by Paul Currie, one of this chapter's heroes.

2011 when somebody entered his cider for CAMRA's National Cider & Perry of the Year competition – and it won!

Laurence was at a crossroads. 'There was no real history of making cider in Middle England,' he said – until he invented one. But here was his dilemma: steady but boring job, or the breathtaking rollercoaster of making his living as an artisan craftsperson? Then in 2012 fate made his mind up for him: he got the elbow from work and was left with nothing but a few bobs' compo. Just enough, as it went, to lease an old canalside sawmill at Wolverton. Hence the new name, Wharf.

By that time Laurence was foraging apples from more than 300 locations in and around Milton Keynes, and his mind was straying not unnaturally to thoughts of apple brandy. A small quantity, contract-distilled by John Walters's English Spirit Company, then based at Dullingham in Cambridgeshire, was followed by the acquisition of a small (and cheap) hand-built pot still from Portugal; and Laurence had lift-off. 'I always fancied trying my hand at dark spirits rather than the usual gin and vodka,' he says; and as well as his own cider 600 litres of imperfect wine from a new vineyard near Buckingham went into the pot. 'Bad wine makes better brandy,' he says, following advice as old as the sixteenth century.

But whisky had always been his favourite, and in keeping with his instinct to co-operate he obtained a wash from the neighbouring Concrete Cow microbrewery and in 2014 laid down his first whisky. But even before the whisky – which was to be bottled as Cattle Creep – had awoken from its three-year obligatory slumber Wharf had to move from Wolverton to a former farm shop in a dairy yard in

Potterspury in Northamptonshire (the suffix being one of a group in the area signifying pear orchards). At the same time the cidermaking had to be knocked on the head and Laurence started concentrating entirely on distilling. Another move was to come following a dispute with the landlord at Potterspury. Wharf operated from several temporary bases for a time, finally coming to rest in 2021 in larger premises in Towcester.

'Gin is our best seller but whisky is our best-selling dark spirit,' he says. 'The darker ones are still my favourites. We had a go at rum but it isn't ready yet. I have always been a whisky buff, and I have always been anti-corporate. I like to think that I produce the antidote.'

He sees innovation and variety as the strength of the artisanal model: grow too big and the necessary economies of scale restrict innovation. 'Whisky is a vintage product, and is not all the same,' he says. 'I have used chocolate and caramalt as a departure from the standard pale malt. We use different yeasts, as well. It's all about the opportunity to do something different. There is so much room for innovation that it's the logical development. For instance, the three-year rule bugs me. It's stifling.'

Wharf's list of whiskies and new makes now resembles the Argos catalogue. As well as Cattle Creep there are two single malts, Solstice and Equinox, in various expressions including one aged in chestnut – the coming thing, by all accounts, as its open grain allows for faster maturation. Then there's Fyr Drenc, the new make, or malt spirit if you prefer; its name is Old English, and why not?

DR JIM SWAN: MIDWIFE OF ENGLISH WHISKY

In the sixteenth century when gin and whisky began to diverge, gin was neutral spirit sold mainly to pharmacists straight off the still as a solvent for their healing herbs whereas whisky was a neutral spirit sold principally to pharmacists as a solvent for their healing herbs but stored in oak for indeterminate periods first. Dr Jim Swan (d. 2017) of Edinburgh, did more than most to unlock the secrets of oak and whisky. His PhD thesis in the late 1960s was about the effect of wood extracts on the maturation of Scotch whisky; and his last published work, in a European technical journal in 1993, was a study of the respective effects of kilning and air-drying on cooperage oak wood.

Dr Swan spent the first years of his career at the Inveresk (later the Pentland) Research Institute, where he developed techniques absolutely critical to the development of a fledgling whisky industry such as England's. As his Scotchwhisky.com obituary put it: 'One of Dr Swan's particular skills – and there were many – lay in enabling start-up distilleries to hit the ground running, using production and maturation techniques to create a spirit that was approachable in youth, but without sacrificing quality.' In other words, how to use oak to make a three-year-old taste like a seven-year-old – an essential tool in the workshop for a business deprived of cash flow.

From the 1990s onwards Dr Swan switched to a more missionary role as a consultant spreading the knowledge he had gained as a researcher to whisky distillery start-ups large and small throughout the world. These included The English Distillery in Norfolk, the first in England to bring a malt whisky to market; so he might indeed be called the midwife of English whisky, although his more widely used nickname is the Einstein of Whisky. Another English venture in which he was deeply involved was the Cotswolds Distillery, whose founder Dan Szor eulogised him fulsomely:

'Our yet-to-be released whisky – and world whisky in general – owes Jim a huge debt,' he said on Scotchwhisky.com. 'As a start-up trying to find our way in the world and develop our own style, we asked Jim for his guidance – and he was instrumental in helping us to optimise our production process and elaborate our wood programme. Some of his most important work included his development of the STR (shaved, toasted and recharred) cask. We have embraced this cask as an important element of our signature style, and every time I taste those resinous, fruity oak notes I will remember his genius.'

Wikipedia summarised Dr Swan's importance thus: 'It was his particular merit to teach young distilleries how to produce whisky in such a way that it reaches maturity and complexity much earlier than usual. His early work on the chemistry of wood helped decipher how different parts of the oak contribute to the flavour of the whiskies. In particular, he was a pioneer and advocate of the STR method for processing red wine barrels.'

A SELECTION OF VILLAINS

Excise duty on beer, cider and spirits was introduced by all three parties to the Civil War in 1643–44 as a temporary fundraiser that proved too useful ever to abolish. Instead, the level of duty and especially the allocation of licences to distil became political footballs used as much to manipulate social policy as to generate cash, but with a deliciously ironical twist. As early as the reign of James I (1603–1625) the dilemma of either levying a high tax on tobacco to deter people from smoking or curbing the tax to make tobacco affordable and maintain government revenue had been observed and commented on with either concern or hilarity. In the end it had to be acknowledged that the government was addicted to tobacco, and so it was to prove with the excise.

TAX AND REGULATION

Mercifully for all concerned, it is not the purpose of this book to detail all the various twists and turns of excise policy over the centuries. But in the volatile periods of the supposed London gin craze of 1720–51 and the much longer-lived problems with unlicensed and untaxed whisky production in western Scotland, sparked by the Union in 1707 and not settled until the 1823 Excise Act, mountainous accretions of regulation, compromise, decree, arbitration, judicial ruling and every other form of quasi-legislation known to or imagined by or susceptible of misconstruction or misinterpretation by bureaucracy began to sprout and clump like mussels on a rope. The mussels themselves, it was found when they were finally prised open, were mostly dead and indeed had never even been alive in that they sprang out of exigency and diktat rather than primary legislation and had never really had any force in law. But when the first revivalist pilgrims entered the Valley of the Shadow of Death they were confronted by the Apollyon HMRC (Her Majesty's Revenue & Customs, the result of the 2005 merger of Her Majesty's Customs & Excise with the Inland Revenue), swirling and swooping on dragon's wings and hurling his fiery bolts of WOWGR [Warehousekeepers and Owners of Warehoused Goods Regulations] of Notices 196 and 197, of duty stamps, of Trade Facility

Warehouses, of Duty Deferment provisions, of premises guarantees... and this is only a taste of the spells and enchantments with which the great demon Jargon sought to confuse and confound the seekers after malt.

To add insult to injury the gin makers, or most of them, were spared the worst of these tortures, for as they bought in their duty-paid base spirit they only needed compounder's licences, which HMRC could not refuse. To be fair the most onerous area of regulation lay and still lies in the warehousing and movement of spirits, where they are at their most vulnerable to... ahem... evaporation. Still, in terms of regulation at least compounding is very much less burdensome than distilling; perhaps that's why by far the majority of newcomers opted for soaking fines herbes (and some juniper) in spirit rather than tackling the altogether thornier business of making whisky from scratch: the perceived difficulty of gaining a licence to distil was just too great a deterrent.

There were happier times to come. The regulation on the minimum size of spirit still, for instance – a preposterously and prohibitively large 1800 litres – was found not to have been authorised by statute after all and could therefore be quietly dropped. Somebody somewhere, it seemed, had persuaded His Majesty's Revenue and Customs (HMRC) that its ambition was not merely to jealously safeguard duty revenue but to promote and advance the promising new sector that was beginning to generate it. HMRC is now charged with giving fair and prompt consideration to all new applications within its overall framework for excise approvals. In the 1980s, however, when Bertram Bulmer and Julian Temperley founded their distilleries, HMCE may have been perfectly accustomed to licensing the new builds, nearly all of them in Scotland, required by big distillery conglomerates whose capacity fluctuated according to world demand but was resistant to the strange idea that any lesser mortal might want a distillery. Allt-a-Bhainne, Auchroisk, Braeval – these applications for new licences in Scotland went through if not exactly on the nod, certainly with a minimum of fuss. That was not the experience of pioneering artisan distilleries south of the Border, though. But from 2000 on the growing clamour for new licences from small artisanal distilleries both in Scotland and down among the sassenachs too, revealed weaknesses in the regime that governed licensing. Where it had seemed monolithic and implacable, it now proved flexible enough to answer the demand. To everyone's astonishment and joy, it proved not merely flexible but – by Civil Service standards, admittedly – positively gymnastic.

What the 1979 Alcoholic Liquor Duties Act, the governing statute, actually stipulated was that HMRC 'may' refuse a licence if the main spirit still had a capacity of less than 1800 litres; but it now became generally agreed that it needed a good reason to refuse a licence and that having a spirit still of less than 1800 litres wasn't good enough. This was a very significant breakthrough which allowed small artisanal distillers such as English Spirit, then based in a former county council highways road-salt depot at Dullingham in Cambridgeshire, to make its astonishing array of short-run spirits. They were made from a variety of its own fermented liquors right through to final product on a set of three 200-litre pot stills. (English Spirit now operates from distilleries in Essex and Cornwall and is mainly a contract distiller producing gin, vodka, rum and liqueurs to order along with the occasional whisky in maximum batches of 100 bottles. The Cornish branch, at Treguddick, is also something of a tourist destination.)

That didn't mean it was suddenly easy to persuade HMRC to agree the licence conditions for an undersized spirit still. Customs was happy enough to grant licences for more or less any size of rectifying still to those who planned to buy in their ethanol; but it took some of the smallest artisan distillers who sought to make their spirits from scratch two years of negotiations before they could satisfy HMRC that they were serious, that they had a viable business plan and that to make small-batch spirits such as grappa, fruit eaux-de-vie, cider brandy and malt whisky that they absolutely needed to make their own wash and their own ethanol. The snail's pace bureaucracy and what some saw as plain obstructionism left a nasty taste in many mouths. Still, if the old 1800 litres cut-off point was still being rigidly enforced, English Spirit could never have come into being. Black Cow vodka is another case in point: its neutral spirit is distilled from fermented whey, a lactose-rich by-product of the award-winning cheesemaking carried on by Jason Barber at Childhay Manor in West Dorset. Clearly, Black Cow had to make its own ethanol; equally clearly, a spirit still of 1800 litres would have been completely unfeasible. But, said Black Cow, once the plan was fully explained HMRC became extremely helpful, shedding its former intransigence and demonstrating a near-puppyish willingness to encourage budding entrepreneurs rather than obstruct them.

THE THREE-YEAR RULE

But if licensing issues had been tamed, there still stood between the putative whisky maker and the actual whisky one giant obstacle: the three-year rule.

The Royal Commission on Whiskey & Other Potable Spirits was commissioned after intense industry lobbying to challenge a court ruling that threatened its very existence. In the 1870s and '80s phylloxera, a voracious vine weevil of American extraction, wrought havoc on the vineyards of Europe. One of its many consequences was the virtual destruction of the various Continental brandy industries; and therein lay a vast opening for the export-quality Scotch and Irish whiskies. But it was going to be a tricky opportunity to exploit. Phylloxera had spread rapidly among a vine population that had had no chance to develop immunity. But whisky production could not easily be expanded quickly enough to compensate: whisky needs its time in oak.

Fortunately the whisky barons had an answer to hand. Legislative reforms in the 1860s had made it possible for grocers to bottle their own stocks of whisky and thus facilitate the take-home trade, which was potentially huge – particularly among the middle classes, who were beginning to prefer drinking in their increasingly comfortable homes among select company to venturing into smelly, smoky saloons where the company could and did encompass all classes and occupations. These bourgeois boozers expected the best and would pay for it, so the potential market for bottled whisky was not only large, it was lucrative. The problem for the grocers was that if you ordered by the barrel whether direct from the distiller or via a broker you never really knew what you were going to get – dark or pale, refined or syrupy, smoky as a dockside dive-bar or fresh as a fairy's undies, benignly mellow or aggressively fiery – and the customers wouldn't stand for it. The answer lay in the continuous or column or patent still, perfected in 1830 from earlier models by an Irish excise officer called Aeneas Coffey and capable via ingenious devilry (explained below) of distilling, cheaply and efficiently, wash brewed from any old cereal.

The Coffey still turned out a continuous stream of near-neutral mixed-grain spirit which, when skilfully and liberally used in blending and homogenising the various and varied vintages of malt, reduced the whole to a consistent quality. Many of these grocers evolved, having perfected the reliability, palatability and affordability of their blends, into full-time bottlers who started branding their whiskies. Usher's Green Label was supposedly the first, but White Horse and others still around today were among them too.

These blends, bottled at six to the gallon and packed in 12 or 24-bottle cases, proved easy to load on to a train in consignments of differing sizes for delivery to English grocers to sell by the bottle

– obvious and easy to us, but a great novelty in the 1860s. Scotch began to catch on in the English market, but only slowly. It was phylloxera and the export opportunity it created that gave Scotch the boost it needed. Soon fine blends and vatted malts were filling the crystal tumblers of every posh restaurant and hotel dining room *sur le continent* where once only French brandy had been good enough, and the English trade picked up accordingly. Then in 1905 Islington Borough Council prosecuted a random publican for passing this off as whisky. The council argued that the end result of blending pure malt whisky with the product of the Coffey still could hardly be called whisky, because it's almost colourless and very bland product was not a different sort of whisky at all but was an adulterant. And adulteration being a very hot topic at the time, the council won.

The subsequent Royal Commission report, published in February 1909 (and using the spelling 'whiskey' throughout), proposed a compromise: if the malt and grain whiskies were both matured in oak barrels for a minimum of three years, it said, they could jointly and severally call themselves whiskey. Or whisky, as preferred. This ruling – even though it was quite simply not true, for grain whisky bears so little relation to pot-distilled single malt that they can scarcely be called cousins, let alone twins – satisfied everybody and is still in force more than a century later.

But it's not only the three-year rule that acts as a financial deterrent to setting out as a whisky rather than a gin or vodka distiller. The capital expenditure required is also greater in that the first thing you need is a brewery and the last thing is a stock of oak barrels, neither of which the white spirit distiller has to fork out for. The whisky pioneers were dismayed to find that one of the mussels we described as encrusting the original statute was a prohibition on making the wash on the same premises as distilling it, a hangover of the bits and pieces of ad hoc rule-mongering that came out of the spurious gin craze. Many of the pioneers were amazed to discover what this relic meant in practice: Julian Temperley's two alembics ambulants, Josephine and Fifi, had to be sited two miles from his cider farm; Penderyn had its wash brought in from Brain's of Cardiff and Healey's from St Austell; Adnams had to build an entirely separate distillery when it had only expected to have to squeeze a bit of kit into its magnificent new brewhouse. The climbdown from this hoary non-regulation coincided with the happy discovery that the minimum still size was legally null, thereby shooting two birds with one bullet and doubly enhancing the gaiety of nations. Establishing a whisky distillery, even in an existing building, requires considerable investment.

ESTABLISHING A WHISKY DISTILLERY

It's possible to spend an absolute fortune on building and equipping a distillery. Many do but they don't have to. The specialised nature, the (often patchy) availability, and the sheer quantity of the equipment required make a distillery start-up, even a modest one, more expensive than a brewery start-up but still very much less expensive (and hopefully far more profitable) than, say, buying a pub. The sky really is the limit. But a more sensible question might be: how little might they have gotten away with? One consultant has put the bare minimum outlay on equipment at £100,000, and one of the many new start-up Scottish malt whisky distilleries has reputedly invested £250,000 just in kit. But could you get away with less? Well, that £100,000 has to cover the best part of a brewery as well as stills and a condenser: a hot liquor tank, a malt mill, a mash tun with sparging arm and mechanised paddle and a fermenting vessel or wash back, although obviously no hop kettle. None of these items are necessarily expensive, but it all adds up. Allow perhaps £10,000 for the brewing equipment; a gin or vodka plant would, of course, be that much cheaper since it will need neither brewery nor wash still. As for the stills themselves, many of them have been imported from Germany, Spain and Portugal where 500-litre vessels are commonplace (the Portuguese are particularly accomplished coppersmiths) for around €20,000 all told which – when you convert it into sterling but then add the VAT – comes rather neatly to about £20,000. Add to this, though, the cost of carriage and a formidable list of accessories including a steam generator and heating coils or jacket, a condenser, a spirit safe, a spirit receiver, and enough oak casks to mature the stuff in, will easily double it. Then there's the bottle-filler and its associated bits and pieces and all the pumps and pipes to connect it all up; the labour to install it all; the label and website designers' fees; office furniture and equipment; enough raw materials and bottles to see you through until the sales start coming in; a cash float for overheads such as rent, wages and utilities... suddenly an outlay of £100,000 is beginning to look conservative.

But no, the biggest villain in the story of English whisky isn't the cash flow or the CapEx: it's the mystique. Gin is easy by comparison. Just order a few litres of contract-distilled pure spirit and a little test still, nip down to the supermarket for some juniper berries and pot-pourri and then lock yourself in your kitchen and play. Somebody will like the final result enough to buy it, so what's to lose? Well, 'easy' is a cheap shot. But it wasn't the teeniest bit daunting for artisan distillers to take on the likes of gin giants Gordon's and Beefeater. The mainstream brands had pretty much squandered what credibility they had thanks to corporate manoeuvres like strength reduction, shifting production from one automated megaplant to another and – sin of sins! – withdrawing Booth's, the last oak-aged brand on the market and my Dad's favourite. I vividly remember being shown, back in the early 1990s, how to make the perfect martini by Salim Khoury of the Savoy, later to be manager of the American Bar there. The only gin he would use was Tanqueray Export because, he said, the rest had had all the character knocked out of them – and if the head stirrer and shaker at the Savoy thought like that, then the sector was wide open to innovators and traditionalists alike. To the artisan distillers in those early days the insipid uniformity of most big gin brands was a positive invitation to experiment. Not just the usual lemon zest and lemon peel but lemon balm, lemon mint, lemon grass, even lemon curd would all be perfectly legitimate, if you liked your gin on the lemony side; any chance shrub or creeper could transition into 'local forage'; a medicinal grist of lungwort, echinacea, coltsfoot, marshmallow root, wintergreen, honey and thyme would still, provided it retained a homeopathic memory of juniper, count as gin. Of a sort. A black Spangle with bite.

Whisky, though, is a beast of an altogether more terrifying aspect. It's not just the intricacy of making the stuff, and the utter command of all departments of equipment, ingredient, process and judgment that are mandatory, it's the dragons of myth that have to be confronted and slain that make it such an awesome challenge. Gin's only myth is the fantasy of the eighteenth-century gin craze in London, which we now know to be an entirely fictitious moral panic deliberately promoted by propagandists from the right wing of the Church of England. Whisky, by contrast, perches on a mountain of myth so high and so steep that no mere English tyro stands a chance of countervailing it. With its bothiemen and gaugers, its ghillies and its lairds, with its snug little distilleries in unexpected glens and its grand rambling ones in awful isolation on high heather moors, with its great pyramids of oak barrels, their adolescent contents passing the years in slumber, whisky is more than just another spirit. It's a culture in itself, wafting a mystique whose charm no product of a unit in an industrial estate on the bleak outskirts of an English rustbelt city can hope to contest, however beautifully made. For real whisky is created as much in folklore as in copper; and

Spirit of Yorkshire distillery with column still on left and pot still on right.

it is a daunting prospect for the newcomer to set himself up against the likes of Glenlivet and Glengoyne and Glenturret and Glen Grant and Highland Park and the quaichful of magic that each bottle contains.

BLUEPRINTS FOR SURVIVAL

The three-year rule may have started life as a consumer protection measure but quickly became one of the industry's proudest boasts. The compulsory ageing of whisky – which has to mature in cask for even longer than cognac – is still seen as a badge of quality rather akin to the German Reinheitsgebot, which prevents the adulteration of beer. But for the parvenu, it puts the brake on cash flow. Gin, vodka and eau-de-vie can start earning their keep the moment they're out of the receiver, but whisky takes its time. A start-up manufacturing company facing a minimum of three years (and in practice much longer, because who can sell such a raw young spirit at any sort of premium?) without earning a penny is pretty much a no-no for any investor. But there are ways round it.

The most obvious is to use some of the equipment and divert a portion of the low wines from the wash still, rectify it with whatever botanicals appeal to you, and bottle it as gin. Or you can dispense with the fruit and veg altogether and bottle it as vodka. Even those who have always seen themselves primarily as whisky distillers aren't above this practice; Dan Szor of Cotswolds, a zealot for whisky, was bottling gin (and damned fine gin at that) for years before his new make could be called whisky.

Diversifying into gin rectification to generate cash flow has become something of a commonplace. There are, however, two more well-trodden paths for whisky distillers seeking to generate cash flow while their stocks slumber in bond.

The first and easiest way is to bottle and sell limited quantities of immature spirit not as whisky (which would be illegal) but as what it is: new make. New make is not ready for drinking, and none of the samples I have, er, enjoyed were really fit to drink unless homeopathically diluted; but as a curio or brand accessory new make is an option with all sorts of advantages. The first is that true aficionados are always eager for something new, and the very existence of your new make will be enough to persuade them to buy it almost whatever the premium. Miniatures of it sell well to collectors, despite being terrible value for money and an absolute swine to bottle. The second is that it complements, rather than detracts from, the marketing of your principal product. It becomes a forerunner, a countdown to the main event, a John the Baptist, as it were. Suffice it to say that it will create anticipation, even suspense, and build a market for your single malt whisky even before it is released. The third is that a full or perhaps 50cl bottle of new make, immature though it be, can command the same price as the whisky it will one day become and the very rarity value keeps the retail price high.

The second method of raising cash, selling casks in bond to amateur investors, used to be regarded as very dodgy indeed, and many of the unwary got stung by the unscrupulous before the practice all but died out. But it has now been rediscovered, and with an added ingredient: honesty. This is the practice of selling maturing stocks in bond to investors long before the contents of the casks are ready for bottling, and once upon a time it was a notorious con. People who'd been promised dizzyingly huge profits on cellars stuffed with fine single malt found either that the stocks didn't exist at all or, if they did, that they were miserable stuff only fit to make anti-freeze with.

The trick for the distiller is not to see the investors as dupes but to build up a personal relationship of trust and even friendship with them. You might buy a whole barrel of your very own, with your name written on it, which you can pop along from time to time to pat, to stroke and to take an investigative sip from, and which will, when the time is exactly right, be bottled for you; or you might buy a share in a particular make and draw a profit from its eventual sale. Either way, the whole experience should be – well, an experience. It's exactly how Cotswolds Distillery funded the construction of its own bonded warehouse, and it's actually how Cotswolds got started in the first place, as we have seen.

A SHORT CHRONOLOGY

Wales has its own thriving whisky industry now, thanks to Penderyn. English whisky most definitely came second in the race. That surely makes Hicks & Healey, the Cornish cidermaker/distiller, the first English whisky distiller then? Oh no it doesn't! Its pot still was filled with a wash brewed by St Austell Brewery in 2003, but the spirit matured in oak for seven years before bottling. First past the post was Norfolk's The English Distillery, built from scratch by the late James Nelstrop, in some corner of a field near Thetford in 2006. Aided and abetted by retired Laphroaig head distiller Iain Henderson, Chapter 6 was laid down in December that year and was bottled exactly three years later. Quite some Christmas present!

The launch of Chapter 6 made headlines on the strength of its novelty value. None of the journalists who wrote it up knew nor could predict how serious the venture was; to many it must have seemed a nine days' wonder. But nobody was left in any doubt the following year that distilling was a very serious business indeed when the Suffolk brewer Adnams installed an entirely new fully computerised brewhouse and turned the old one into the Copper House distillery. The much-loved but apparently sleepy old family firm was in the throes of complete reinvention by a new generation of the ruling dynasty. Simon Loftus and Jonathan Adnams had already delivered a world-beating, carbon-free warehouse; the distillery came about in pursuance of a policy of achieving sustainability through maximising the potential of the home site and its locality. Much of the grain used in the distillery is grown on Jonathan Adnams's farm less than two miles away; more comes from Holkham Hall across the border in Norfolk; and the whole lot is malted in Bury St Edmunds. Vodka and gin were Copper House's first products; but in 2011 it was decided to use the stills' down days to make whisky as well, basing the various brands on all sorts of grain including wheat, rye and oats as well as barley.

The arrival of Adnams on the nascent English whisky scene was a game-changer. English whisky moved from the margins to the mainstream. Heavyweight investment became, if not the norm, an ever-present possibility. Brexit and Covid wrought their damage here as everywhere. But partly because English whisky inhabits the top shelf, far above the high-tide mark of economic catastrophe and political myopia, and partly because of the determination and, to use an overworked cliché, the passion of its protagonists, English whisky lives among us and will do so for as long as the weary world grinds on.

AVENGERS ASSEMBLE!

English whisky's biggest problem is that few people know or even believe that it exists. It's an identity crisis on a grand scale and in 2021 two of the biggest practitioners of the art, Dan Szor of Cotswolds and Andrew Nelstrop of The English Distillery, decided not unreasonably that the best way to tackle it was together.

It was a timely decision: the EU Directive defining various spirits was due to lapse by the end of 2023 and DEFRA – the Department of the Environment, Food, & Rural Affairs, or the plain old Min of Ag as was –

was starting consultations on what should fill the ensuing legislative vacuum. This was the opportunity to raise the flag of English whisky – and not only that: it was the last chance to set standards in a sector that was growing large enough to invite the attention of predators who might not be as scrupulous about quality as the pioneers. So Dan and Andrew got on the blower and did a quick ring-round. Fourteen of the 40 answered the call, and the English Whisky Guild (EWG) was born.

DEFRA was faced with a number of options for the regulation of whisky distilling post-Brexit, ranging from a whole new statute with all the Parliamentary whistles and bells to a simple statutory order nodded through by the Secretary of State establishing a new Geographical Indicator (GI) – you know, the rule that says things like 'to call yourself a Melton Mowbray pork pie you must be made in Melton Mowbray' and 'to call yourself Stilton cheese you may not come from Stilton'; and since the latter was the cheaper the latter it would be.

The work of putting together the GI application was led by Oxford Artisan Distillery's Tagore Ramoutar, who had the delicate task of drawing up a proposal for a regulatory framework that protected the best of traditional (in effect, Scottish) practice without compromising the freedom of action that many English artisan distillers were already enjoying and wanted to preserve. Not unnaturally there was little dissent among EWG members that the GI should specify the exclusive use of grains grown and malted in the UK. With localism such a common article of faith, English whisky distillers by and large already use all-English malted barley anyway; but the Guild is ready to stretch the point a little to allow for mainly Scottish specialities such as peated malt that English producers do not customarily supply.

Other points in the GI application have not been so universally welcomed. For instance, those who have been experimenting with speeding maturation by combining smaller casks with oak chips or spindles or by other means will be disappointed: the Guild intends to stick by the three-year rule. Many maintain that skilful manipulation of the area of contact between oak and spirit reduces the maturation time required without harming the flavour, and they are quite probably right; but if they try it the finished product may not be called whisky. Or whiskey. Or even *chwisgi*. It's a hard call for the Guild: we know that historically the rule was an anti-adulteration measure; but as with the Reinheitsgebot it has become a badge of quality which it would be impossible to withdraw from. As a consolation, though, the Guild proposal allows for the use of woods other than oak, provided it is made quite clear on all labelling.

Then there's the question of stills. The Guild would be happy for the GI to allow single malts to be made in copper pot stills with rectifying columns, like the existing Lomond and Faraday stills. But English single malts may not be made on untraditional stills – stainless steel, for instance, or vacuum stills. This has prompted one great innovator, Liam Hirt of Bristol's Circumstance Distillery, to drop out of the Guild altogether: copper, he maintains, does not affect the quality of the product, and the Guild's GI application means that English whisky will forever remain in the shadow of Scotch. Frustratingly, DEFRA is scheduled to make its decision just after this book goes to press.

Even though the first item on its agenda has been a piece of fairly heavyweight lobbying, the Guild was never envisaged as primarily a lobbying organisation. It is, insists chairman Andrew Nelstrop, first and foremost promotional, agreeing and adhering to certain standards that will create and maintain a reputation for excellence. To quote its manifesto:

'We support a community of producers by sharing achievements and learning for the future good of English whisky. We are working to define clearly the technical standards for what constitutes English whisky and monitor adherence to those standards, and we will propagate all agreed standards so that they are known, understood and accessible to all current and prospective producers and anyone with an interest in English whisky.

'We build interactions with producers of all sizes to champion our sector and strive to operate both our business and our whisky production in as sustainable and environmental manner as possible, with a focus on reducing our carbon footprints.

'We build awareness of the English whisky category with all whisky drinkers and prospective whisky drinkers and all interested in the health and future of English whisky. We share who we are, what we stand for, and how our whiskies are crafted meticulously from grain to glass and will create platforms and spaces for drinkers to discover, enjoy and learn about English whisky both face-to-face and virtually.'

The Guild appointed Morag Garden as CEO in 2023 and will be taking English whisky to trade and consumer shows at home and abroad. So if the early days of the Guild have not been without dissension, we can now say that the sector has a united voice and will go on to create a single big, glittering, glaring shop window the world cannot ignore.

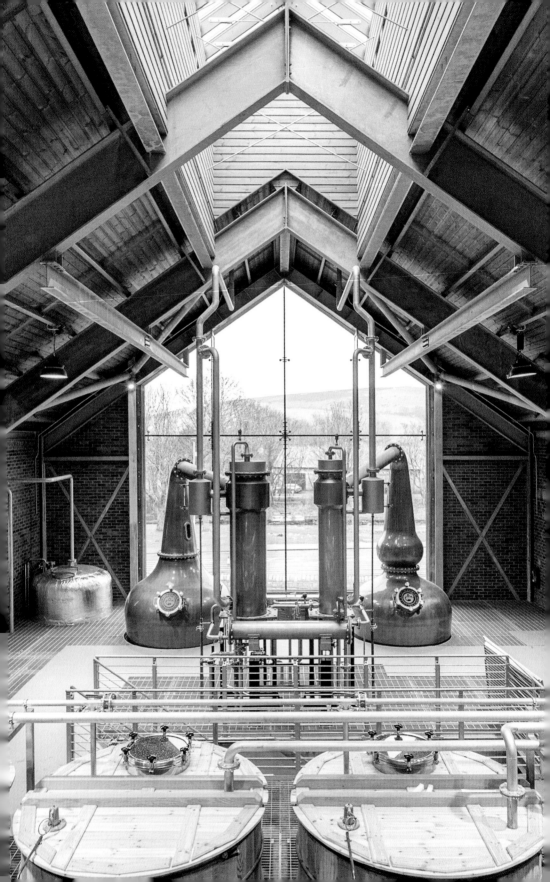

NEW WHISKY DISTILLERIES

2003
Hicks & Healey, Cornwall.

2006
English Whisky Company, Norfolk. (now called The English Distillery)

2008
Ludlow, Craven Arms, Shropshire.

2010
Adnam's Copper House, Suffolk.

2011
Canterbury Brewers & Distillers, Kent.

Wharf, Northamptonshire.

2014
Cotswolds, Warwickshire.
Dartmoor, Devon.
Durham, Co Durham.
East London Liquor Company, London.
Forest, Cheshire.
Isle of Wight Distillery, Isle of Wight.
The Lakes, Cumbria.

2015
Brightwell Bottle, Oxfordshire.
Bimber, London.
Colwith Farm, Cornwall.
Princetown, Devon.
The Wrecking Coast, Cornwall.

2016
Cooper King, North Yorkshire.
Copper Rivet, Kent.
Doghouse, London.
Pocketful of Stones, Cornwall.
Spirit of Yorkshire, North Yorkshire.
White Peak, Derbyshire.

2017
Henstone, Shropshire.
Old Bakery, London.
The Oxford Artisan Distillery, Oxfordshire.

2018
Circumstance, Bristol.
Yarm, Durham.

2019
Elsham Wold, Lincolnshire.
Retribution, Somerset.
Weetwood, Cheshire.
West Midlands, Birmingham.
Whittaker's, North Yorkshire.

2020
Mercia, Staffordshire.
Wiltshire Whisky, Wiltshire.

2021
Spirit of Birmingham, Birmingham.
Ten Hides, Wiltshire.

2022
Ad Gefrin, Northumberland.

Inside the still house at Ad Gefrin distillery.

CHAPTER THREE

THE LIE OF THE LAND

DOES TERROIR REALLY MATTER?

'What makes English whisky the best, or potentially the best, in the world? The weather. Well, the climate, which is almost the same thing. Oh, and the soil.'

Fields of barley surrounding Spirit of Yorkshire Distillery.

There is an anecdote I have often used, but whose provenance I have completely forgotten, to the effect that Good Queen Bess once berated a boastful Spanish ambassador (this would be before the Armada, I imagine) who was praising the noble wines of his country and denigrating English ale as fit only for peasants. The Virgin Queen reminded him that he had drunk plenty of her ale without finding fault, because it was brewed only from Hertfordshire barley whose malt was as sweet and as exquisite as any Spanish grape. The barley strains of north-western Europe, and especially of the sheltered and temperate eastern half of Great Britain, are every bit as well adapted both to their environment and to their purpose as any grape from any vineyard in any country of the world.

Barley's current state of near-perfection is the result of careful selection by generation upon generation of farmers, seedsmen and, more recently, laboratory-based agronomists. Funny how when an agronomist creates a new strain it's a Frankenstein's monster, but when a horny-handed son of the soil does much the same, it's ancient wisdom; but whatever your view of the genetic manipulation of food crops, those same horny-handed farmers started practising their ancient wisdom on wild barley somewhere in the Middle East around 11,000 years ago. Within no more than a few millennia they found that wheat and barley complemented each other admirably to create between them the ideal all-purpose, year-round foodstuff. Suffice it to say that barley gave birth to malt, and as barley could thrive in temperatures and terrains from Cairo to Caithness that pretty much meant beers all round.

'THE RAIN IT RAINETH ON THE JUST' IS THE FARMER'S PRAYER

This is what makes English whisky the best, or potentially the best, in the world. The weather. Well, the climate, which is almost the same thing. Oh, and the soil.

The counterintuitive and indeed astounding revelation that there is actually something good about the English weather is authoritative. It comes from grain merchant supremo and owner of Wiltshire's

Warminster Maltings: Robin Appel, who with more than 30 years at the forefront of his trade today supplies about half of England's whisky distillers with their malted barley. Robin agrees wholeheartedly with the proposition that English barley is the best in the world, and it's not just empty jingoism on his part.

Barley is pretty mellow stuff. Treated right, it yields a nice plump grain with a big starchy endosperm eager to be transmogrified into fermentable sugar; enough diastatic enzymes to do the transmogrifying with power left over to saccharify an extra charge of unmalted grain; and a hull soft enough to surrender sweetly to the roller's kiss but still spiky enough to curry-comb the liquor till it shines. (It also makes soft straw for animal bedding, but that's by the by.) But it has to be treated right – it likes moderate conditions with just enough sunshine and rain – not too little, not too much – and a fairly even temperature all through the year. Just enough sun to warm without burning; just enough rain to moisten without soaking; just enough snow, if any, to go out and play in.

This ideal can only be relied on in maritime zones of which, as Robin points out, there are precisely five in the entire world. These are New Zealand, the western coast of Canada, the flat coastal parts of Belgium, the whole of Denmark, and the low-lying eastern parts of Scotland and England together with south central England; and of these, the first four are not huge growers of malting barley. They supply enough for their own needs, and much of it is pretty good stuff; but you don't encounter that many trucks of Danish or Flemish malt heading inland from the seaports of China and Brazil. (Not that Robin really approves of exporting bulk malt in its unfermented and undistilled condition: 'It's too good for that,' he maintains. 'To achieve its full value it should only be allowed to leave the country in a bottle.')

And of course, other countries produce malting barley too, millions of tons of it; but their climates are continental rather than maritime. In continental summers much hotter than ours, says Robin, the plants can become baked; while in the wetter winters they can be frozen or drowned or both. European malt is hard-skinned and tough to mill; it's rich in nitrogen and deficient in diastatic enzymes and requires (or required, for science usually finds a way of outflanking nature) the brewer to mash it by the clumsy, time-consuming and energy-inefficient decoction method.

British barley, then, is the best in the world; but English barley is better than Scottish and again, it's down to the weather. Put simply, Scotland is rainier than England; and the growing season is shorter too. Longer days mean that the hours of sunshine each grain can bask in are roughly equal; but that takes no account of all the dreich, schmirr, fret, haar and other fine gradations of atmospheric moisture that are necessary up there. As a result they have historically had to cut the grain while still green and stook it or rick it like hay, throwing the rain off the surface while building up a good old fug at the core to keep the ripening process going. Just like an old-fashioned hayloft, there was a double hazard of mildew from the damp and spontaneous combustion from the heat while the cut crop awaited threshing before finishing off in the corn-dryer. Clearly a most unsatisfactory state of affairs.

English malt is therefore and is hereby officially proclaimed the best; but what is the best of the best? It is, says Robin, that which is blessed enough to grown on an Icknield Series soil type – richly fertile light loam, well-drained and easily tilled, overlaying a bed of absorbent chalk, which retains sufficient water but, spongelike, expels any surplus.

The chalk regulates and makes consistent the moisture content of the soil. England's swathes of Icknield Series soils stretch from Dorset to the Wash in the lee of low but extensive ranges of hills including Dartmoor, the Cambrian Mountains with their lone and lovely outlier, the Malverns, the Cotswolds, the hills of South Shropshire, and the Staffordshire and Derbyshire Peaks. These break the force of the Atlantic gales and soak up the worst of its downpours, producing in the country to their east just enough sun to warm without burning; just enough rain to moisten without soaking; just enough snow, if any, to go out and play in. Yes, there is snow in Norfolk and frost in Cambridgeshire, but it is very seldom very cold, and the winter barley slumbers very snugly.

FACING UP TO CLIMATE CHANGE

Not everything in the garden is lovely, though. Over the course of the last 30-odd years English grape growers have found that many parts of the east and south-east of the country, as well as possessing the same soil types and topography as the Champagne region in eastern France, are also acquiring its climate. Great news for English wine. Not so great for barley growers. Says Robin: 'It's getting drier and drier. We have contract growers all over the country and in East Anglia the harvest is not as plump as it was. And that's the result of climate change.'

Climate change is perhaps intractable as far as individual growers are concerned. All they can do is join the environmental lobby whole-heartedly. But they can also – as, increasingly, they do – renounce the isolation and the conservativism that have come with decades of enslavement by giant agricultural corporations. These corporations have for years been developing new strains of all sorts of crops with the focus on profit rather than flavour. So they might be selected for higher yields and greater resistance to disease, for longer stalks for easier harvesting, or tougher skins to deter pests, or more sugar and less acid to boost their appeal to the infantile palates of the masses, or all of these things; but the development and enhancement of flavour compounds – and malting barley has 50 of them – are, says Robin, pretty much an afterthought.

In tests conducted by the Brewing Research Foundation in 2007–08 bitter and astringent off-flavours were detected in the then number one spring barley, Tipple. Meanwhile heritage varieties Maris Otter and Plumage Archer faced extinction because of low yields until Robin stepped in and bought the rights, promoting them on quality rather than quantity. They were big favourites with small to medium brewers for their biscuity qualities; but supplies could be patchy because growers shrank from devoting enough acreage to them. But then they were approved for distilling, and the maths suddenly changed. Artisan-distilled whiskies are top-shelf products and need to source the best ingredients – or should that be, only the finest ingredients? – to justify their astronomical price-tags. At this level of spend, a high retail price is often far from being a deterrent – rather the opposite, in fact. On the old principle that you wouldn't buy a Rolls Royce for a fiver, cost becomes conflated with value, and the consequent flexibility in retail price creates a frisson all down the supply chain. Better malt – only the finest malt, in fact – is a sine qua non, and if that means a few quid extra then so be it. The customer – that's you, that is – will cough up gladly.

Trade demand for heritage malts has therefore shot up, and independent maltsters like Robin are very happy to see it. But one trend that Robin doesn't see much future for is the use of coloured and specialist brewer's malts – brown, amber, crystal, black – in whisky-making. Rye, of course, is another matter altogether, with its own history and traditions which deserve separate treatment; one or two English whisky distillers have brought out rye whiskies and more will doubtless follow. One of two whisky distillers have had success with judicious additions of chocolate and other coloured or brewer's malts, and Rauchmalz could yet have its day. But, says

English barley being grown in the fields near Spirit of Yorkshire Distillery.

Robin: 'Whisky's flavour comes mostly from the wood, so I can't think why whisky distillers would want to use coloured malts. We have 20-odd distillers getting their supplies from Warminster and none of them are ordering coloured malts.'

In short: if it ain't broke, don't fix it. But then on the other hand, a good prod in the ribs will wake a slumbering lion.

MALTSTERS AND MALTINGS

It's been a cause of constant surprise over the years how little most people know about malt. Perhaps they don't realise how much of it they ingest – in beer, of course; in whisky and in gin as well; in malt loaf and other baked goods including bagels and Rich Tea biscuits; as a coating for tablets; in sweets such as Maltesers; in breakfast cereals; in certain proprietary hot drinks that you don't discover are nothing at all like coffee until after you've taken a sip, when politeness obliges you to finish the whole damned mug. Malt extract used to be given to children in the days of rationing as a source of calories and B vitamins; but eventually it was decided that coating children's teeth with sugar was on balance probably not a good idea. It was also wondered how much of it was being abstracted for home brewing, which was then illegal. But you can see from all these uses what valuable and versatile stuff it is, and you have to wonder how come so few people seem to know what it is. Public confusion might be down to the fact that every town in England has a shopping arcade, an arts centre or a multi-storey car park called The Maltings, which only goes to show how much beer we used to get through.

Malt is the result of fooling barley into thinking it's spring – not all that impressive a feat for, as Ian Dury has it, you can baffle a blockhead with ease – upon which it starts to germinate. The process begins by converting the starches into sugar, intended by nature to feed the growing plant while its roots develop but easily diverted to other uses. How this sleight of hand was discovered is a matter of conjecture – lots and lots of conjecture, in fact – but it's usually said that Stone Age man or woman stumbled across it by accident. Here are two conjectures. One is that grain has to be dried, which if the sun is insufficient requires a low fire. Whoever is meant to be turning the still-damp grain is called away or falls asleep; the grain overheats and scorches; and when it is eventually milled is found to be sweet. This is considered a marvel, because the only other source of sweetness in the area is well-protected by horrid buzzing stinging things, and since sweetness is highly prized malt is an instant hit. Another conjecture is that the baskets were commonly buried in the earth as rat-proof and rainproof granaries might not have been all that rainproof after all. Water got in somehow; and the wet grain, once dug up, was dried and found to have become sweet. Alternatively, the act of sprouting being a thermodynamic reaction, the grain in its near-airtight basket got hotter and hotter until it simply ran out of fuel and put itself out, having saccharified itself the while. For the sweetness of the malt, especially if it was used to make either gruel or a sweet broth for the toothless young and old and for the sick, immediately aroused the interest of loitering micro-organisms such as yeast. Hence, willy-nilly, ale.

Arable and mixed farms from time immemorial each possessed a small malting-floor, which might well have doubled as a grain-dryer: they are, after all, pretty much identical. In a traditional – not to say prehistoric – floor maltings, ripe grain is soaked in a pit or a tun until it swells by about 25 per cent and begins to sprout acrospires or rootlets (little Sir John's 'long, long beard' of John Barleycorn fame). The damp grain is then heaped evenly on a stone floor with a low charcoal fire (or, after the late seventeenth-century deforestation crisis, coke) in a pit underneath it, in a low rectangular louvred chamber in which the humidity can be regulated. The grain is regularly turned by towing or pushing a trolley-like affair spiked with tines or, on smaller floors, a modified rake or just a large shovel. Temperature is critical, and the maltster (the suffix suggesting that the work was originally done by women) has to control it by raking the grain into deeper or shallower piles as required. It was backbreaking work demanding keen judgment and intense concentration, and must have been fuelled (or so one hopes) by plentiful jacks or cans – medieval drinking vessels – of small ale. These days there are only a handful of floor maltings left, the vast majority having been displaced by huge automatic steeping and drying devices, all laden with thermometers, humidity monitors and gas detectors like Marley's Ghost in its chains (but none of them, according to people who prefer the old ways, equipped with the eye of a bloke who scrutinises not only the piece but also its particles). The dried grain is ground into a coarse flour or grist, dunked in a bath of hot but not boiling water, regularly stirred with a mash paddle, and strained; the resulting syrup or wort is then pitched with yeast. In digesting the sugar, the friendly fungus emits carbon dioxide and alcohol, and when it has stopped foaming, you have ale ready either to drink or to distil.

The proliferation of maltings on farms, in castles and monasteries, in villages and towns inevitably led to a wide spectrum of kilning times according to the various preferred materials, methods, degrees of skill, and personal and local customs. Pale malts were always preferred, but the variations in timing and temperature, even in the same batch, could be enormous, running through light gold to reddish to nearly black to downright burnt. Nothing went to waste in thriftier times, and the malt might be sifted and graded to produce vastly different beers. By the time coke, which burns more evenly and controllably than charcoal, became the normal fuel for malt-drying, drinkers had settled firmly on their preferences, and the production of malts of different colours and flavours graduated from the haphazard to the deliberate and highly skilled. For strictly speaking, and thrown in here merely to complicate matters, malt isn't a discrete substance at all. Just as a balti isn't really a curry at all but the miniature wok which in certain regions of India (well, Birmingham, which you can tell by the climate is not actually in India but which seems to have acquired some of the best things about it) is commonly used to cook curries in, so malt or more properly malting is the process by which the insoluble starch in cereal grains is converted into sugar that yeast can get at. Just about any grain can be and is malted, but barley has a particular attribute that makes it the grain of choice for fermentation: it is oversupplied with the diastatic enzymes A-amylase and B-amylase, which are responsible for the

Turning the floor malting with a wooden shiel at Warminster Maltings.

process of saccharification. Saccharification (or in Greek, diastasis; or in English, conversion) continues while the malt flour is being stirred in hot water. This is why you never boil your mash: boiling breaks the amylase down and all you're left with is hot, partly converted mash. Barley's inbuilt surplus of these enzymes means that if added to a mash of 80 per cent maize, wheat, hulls and husks and (as a former Brakspear boss once characterised the ingredients of British-brewed lager) broken biscuit and old bus tickets, it will have the diastatic muscle to make the whole mess sweet enough to ferment.

There are dozens and dozens of malted and unmalted grains and other fermentable adjuncts that are commonly used in brewing: one of my earlier books included an attempt at a compendium of brewing ingredients, and I gave up at nearly 100 malted and unmalted grains and other adjuncts often pitched into the brewer's mash-tun. Actually, most of the malts you meet in beer are standard pale ale or lager malts. Similarly, there is really only one category you will normally find in your whisky; and although each distillery will have malty idiosyncracies of its own, here is the compendium entry for the standard version:

DISTILLER'S MALT

Standard Distiller's or Pot-still malt is very high in nitrogen compared to beer malts. Since distillers are well aware that it's not beer they're producing, the malts they use are bred for maximum efficiency both in terms of their extraction of fermentable sugars and their speed of fermentation. Distiller's malt, therefore, features a high nitrogen content to keep the yeast well-fed and exceptional diastatic power, which enables the distiller to experiment with a high proportion of unmalted grains (because Distiller's malt is high enough in diastatic enzymes to use in a Coffey still).

Scotch whisky makers have tended to be fairly conservative in the matter of malt. Too much is at stake, and malt is so much at the heart of the whole business that innovative distillers have tended to focus their attention more on oaking and maturation, as we shall see. That's not to say that agronomists and distillers don't play around as much as they do in other fields of farming. Golden Promise, for example, was raised by Simpson's Malt, a fifth-generation family firm with maltings in Northumbria and Norfolk, as a new variety of spring-sown malting barley back in the 1960s and proved popular with distillers. However, both yield and resistance to disease were poor by today's standards, and by the 1980s farmers were switching to more profitable newcomers. At that point it was discovered by Caledonian Brewery in Edinburgh and became the base malt for its eponymous best-selling pale ale. Other brewers also took it up and Simpson's put some investment behind it. Although tagged as a 'heritage variety' it's still fairly widely grown for the sort of brewers who don't settle for broken biscuits and old bus tickets.

But the charge against Scottish distillers of conservatism, even over caution, in matters of malt ignores an enormous elephant in the room – a mammoth, even: peat. Peat is no more than turf and its cargo of vegetation, sodden and submerged over millennia on its long journey to becoming coal. Cut and dried, it is flammable but not wildly so and has fuelled the home fires of much of Scotland and Ireland for as long as there have been humans there – which is, ever since the ice receded some 12,000 years ago. With its slow, even burn and aromatic smoke, peat proved ideal for drying sprouting malt. The

Distiller's malts from left to right, Laureate, Black, Maris Otter and Rye.

smoke also conferred a different character on the malt according to the flora it had once supported – trees, grasses, herbs, heather, they each bring their own flavours, which also come, albeit more mildly, through to the whisky from the burns that trickle through the bog.

The phenolic element in peat smoke has a strong medicinal tang that novice whisky drinkers often find off-putting. This can range tremendously from one peated whisky to another depending on the phenol parts per million. This is a calculation of how much phenol content the malted barley has before going to the mash house.

CHOCOLATE, CARAMEL, BUTTERSCOTCH

English whisky distillers have already shown their propensity for experimentation in that a number of them have created whiskies using that most un-English of cereals, rye. Rye's historical heartland has always been the north German, Polish and Ukrainian plains where summer can be as temperate as it likes but winter is reliably ferocious, and shelter from its icy blasts is there none. One of rye's outstanding characteristics is that not only can it withstand several degrees of frost, but it also outcompetes winter-hardy weeds, breaking up impacted soil and nitrogenating it. The Dutch imported a lot of it in the sixteenth and seventeenth centuries when their urban populations were burgeoning but attempts at getting enough grain to feed them from swampy and flood-prone soils were literally floundering. In the early years of the seventeenth century they founded the trading post of New Orange on the Hudson River in the eastern USA, later expanding their territory, renaming the colony New Netherland, and founding the city of New Amsterdam. A sizeable population of farmers arrived from overcrowded Holland, bringing rye with them, and stayed on after the British takeover of 1664, renaming the city as New York. Subsequent British colonists saw the value of rye in a land where winters were just as fierce as in northern Europe; and the Irish and Scots in later generations of migrants seized on its potential for distillation, finding its behaviour in washback and pot very similar to barley's. Rye whiskey was soon a staple of American distilling along with other adaptations and acclimatisations, such as Bourbon, sour mash, corn and others; and rye has now been picked up by English whisky distillers including Adnams, Oxford Artisan and the late lamented City of London. Perhaps, given the sophistication of Britain's maltsters, working with the huge range of kilnings available here will one day become the English whisky industry's peculiar hallmark. Scott Ferguson at Eden Mill (in Scotland) has dared to try out various brewing malts – 50kg of chocolate malt added to 800kg of Golden Promise left a lingering mocha, while 25kg each of brown and crystal created warm flavours of toast and shortbread. 'I was surprised by how well the flavours carried through,' said Scott. 'I'm also surprised that more distillers haven't tried out different malts. Glenmorangie did it with chocolate malt and it worked brilliantly.'

English whisky makers are indeed coming round to the idea of washes that hybridise ancient brewing and distilling mashing practices, sometimes using very hefty doses of coloured malts to counteract the fact that distilling subtracts from base flavours. A hopped version of Spirit of Birmingham's Black Mash sells well in its own right. So: Cornish crystal malt whisky, anyone?

TERROIR

Britain's artisan distillers have much to thank the microbrewing industry for, not least several scrapyards-worth of outgrown, outworn and fire-sale vessels and pipework in usable condition, for which see below. But in this instance we are looking at nothing so tangible. We are looking at a concept, and we are looking at an argument.

Until the early years of this century farmers sold their barley to maltsters in bulk, as a commodity graded according to its content of desirable components such as carbohydrates. But the farmers – unaccountably skint, as always – were fed up, in the words of one of them, of getting feed prices for premium malting barley and were always on the lookout for new ways to optimise the value of their crop. Then, in Norfolk, a cabal of farmers, maltsters and microbrewers had a very topical 'Good Idea'. In these days of localism and provenance the fact that a bag of malt might contain grain from anywhere in the world be it Barley, Hertfordshire, or Bali, Indonesia, did nothing for the esteem in which it was held or the price it could command. Traceability was the thing, so said Gary Rhodes and all the other TV chefs; so instead of jumbling up all the different loads of grain straight off the lorry and processing them indiscriminately as they arrived, the smaller independent maltsters with their inverted economy of scale separated the incoming barley farm by farm, even field by field so that a sack of malt could reliably be labelled according to its place of origin. It suited the participating farmers who now had an incentive to grow a better crop; it suited the small maltsters because it was something their bigger and more industrialised competitors simply couldn't do; and it suited the microbrewers because it gave them malt of unmatched quality and could be cited as proof to consumers that they cared about every last little detail, however small.

Traceability on such a scale was a notion that appealed on cultural grounds not only to craft brewers but to artisan distillers as well; but it also prompted debate as to the actual organoleptic advantage of such intense micro- or even nano-management, and it introduced a new word to the UK distilling industry: terroir. The word or at any rate the concept it embraces came from the vineyards of France to the barley fields of Britain thanks to the advocacy of one of the independent distilling's superstars, Mark Reynier. A wine merchant by trade and the possessor of the most formidable set of papillae you are ever likely to be humbled by, Reynier was one of a consortium of independent distilling superstars, which in 2000 bought the Bruichladdich distillery on Islay from Whyte & Mackay after it had spent six years in mothballs. The consortium in turn sold Bruichladdich to Rémy Martin in 2012 – Reynier himself dissenting – by which time it had turned the once-unloved plant (still equipped with its largely original equipment) into a witch's cauldron of innovation and experiment. Reynier went on to found the Waterford Distillery in Ireland and the Renegade rum distillery on Grenada and to elaborate his ideas about, among other things, the importance of terroir to the artisan distiller.

Now, we all know that French intellectuals have a soft spot for grandiloquence: as my (admittedly rather cynical) French A-level teacher once said: *L'être ou le néant* or 'Being and Nothingness', the title of a book by Jean-Paul Sartre, sounds terribly important – until you translate it. Is the same thing true of terroir?

To a vigneron or French grape grower, no. To a vigneron, terroir means the composition and condition of the soil, degrees latitude, elevation and aspect of the plot, average rainfall and prevalent winds of the district, local microflora and fauna, and any variation thereof that might have any bearing on the eventual fruit. The aberrant patch of clay at the top of the vineyard gives that corner a terroir all of its own. To such a meticulous vigneron, the fact that half of his holding faces south-west and the other half faces west-south-west means it makes two different wines, while the notion of Burgundy is far, far too wide to have any practical meaning at all. It's all very French – as Reynier himself hinted at, when in an interview with Christopher Coates of *Whisky Magazine*, he explained terroir in English. 'Of course, farmers here don't call it terroir – they call it farming,' he said. 'And gardeners, who understand that roses must be planted on a south-facing slope to thrive, or that soil pH will determine how particular plants will grow, call it gardening.' In more spiritual terms, though, it means for him and those who follow the same line of thought an unbreakable bond between farmer and maltster; it means organic and even biodynamic cultivation.

This all sounds admirable and (apart from the biodynamic bit) hard to argue with. Indeed, it's a fact of quotidian life for thousands of viticulturalists and winemakers all over the world. But how is it relevant to the English artisan distiller? There is, after all, a conceptual opposition between winemaking, which aims to express the character of variety and vintage, and whisky distilling, which aims for a consistent blend of malt and oak of many different provenances. Add to that the degree of processing the grain goes through compared to the grape – malting, mashing, fermenting, distilling, maturing and finishing, often in a succession of variously conditioned barrels, as opposed to pressing and fermenting alone – and it is hard to imagine that much if any of the barley's original distinctive character is going to shine through in the glass. Not that barley, even of different strains, has much of a distinctive character in the first place. And you certainly wouldn't expect anything in the way of terroir from a big-brand blend of whisky such as Bell's or Famous Grouse. Like cognac, homogenised from the output of hundreds of small vineyards, these are the results of the blender's peculiar skill, and the myriad individual hints, notes and suggestions have all been drowned... in each other.

For the artisan distiller it's a different matter. Those who grow their own barley like Spirit of Yorkshire or who maintain a very close relationship with their supplier like Cotswolds might not share Reynier's passion in its entirety; but they do share the spirit and they do see its value. But perhaps in their case it's more to do with ethos and identity than with the flavour in the bottle. Surely only one in a million consumers have tastebuds sharp enough to detect the kind of qualities that Mark Reynier can, especially in spirits. I once went to a Calvados tasting and after three or four samples it became an exercise in futility (although definitely not a waste of time). Perhaps that's why so many in the industry think terroir is bunkum, an attitude encapsulated by Fine & Rare blogger Holly Motion: 'We see terroir being bandied about by craft distillers who want to sell their inconsistencies as something intentional, rather than the result of lack of craftsmanship,' she says. 'To those I say: get some proper training and purchase some proper equipment and try to produce some consistent quality drinks. Consistency is the precursor to quality. Inconsistency does not equal a claim to terroir. It usually just signals minimal process control.'

But perhaps the last word should go to Reynier, again quoted by Coates and following some recent research on terroir in Texas. 'There aren't 100 flavour compounds in whisky, as previously thought,' he says. 'There are 2000; and 60 per cent of them are influenced by where the barley grows. Terroir exists.'

SUSTAINABILITY

Arguments as to the importance of terroir to the English artisan distiller may be a bit abstruse for many; but related considerations, particularly where the environment is concerned, certainly aren't. Culturally, artisan distillers belong firmly in the ethical, mindful, aware camp: they are 'woke', as somebody who knows what if anything the word means might dismiss them. This is where traceability comes into it: the distiller will want to know not only whether the malt is organic but also that it was grown on a farm with hedgerows and spinneys where wildlife might peacefully co-exist, on soil that isn't being pounded solid by agricultural behemoths the size of houses, on land where the hunt has never set hoof and where coverts and thickets remain untroubled by 12-bores and beaters.

Central to all this is energy. Of course it makes sense for everybody, given the expense, to use as little energy as they can get away with; but distilling is a particularly energetic business. Not just in the sense of hauling whole harvests of barley up and down the country, then malting and milling it before loading it back on the lorry for its journey to the distillery, which is all energy-consuming enough as well as horribly polluting; but also in the sense of bringing countless litres of wort up to mashing temperature, holding it there while the sugars are extracted, cooling it down to pitching temperature, then heating it up again in the still, then... So you can see why both proximity and cleaner, cheaper energy (and less of it) are priorities.

And then, too, 90 per cent of the water and 10 per cent of the grain used in the process ends up as waste. Simple waste reduction measures such as feeding spent grain to livestock and using the protein-rich pot ale left after distillation as a soil conditioner have long been the norm.

But during World War II tentative efforts at mitigating the industry's immense waste of energy started when Deanston distillery was converted to hydroelectric power. In the 1970s Glen Garioch briefly used its waste heat to warm greenhouses, while since 1990 Bowmore's waste heat has made a tropical spa of the swimming pool in the leisure centre in one of its old warehouses. Scottish distillers have worked hard with the Government to continue and advance these measures: by 2012, the industry had cut its CO_2 emissions by 10 per cent on 2008 levels, despite an 11 per cent increase in production. Meanwhile, its energy consumption had grown by little more than 1 per cent, and the proportion of energy derived from non-fossil sources had increased from 3 per cent to 16 per cent.

In 2013–14 oil-burning boilers were replaced with woodchip-fired generators at Tomatin, Aberfeldy, Balmenach and Royal Brackla. A £30 milion plant opened at Rothes by Diageo, Chivas Brothers, Inver House, Edrington Group, Glen Grant and BenRiach generates 7MW and saves 47,000 tonnes in CO_2 emissions a year, while Diageo's new £40 million distillery at Roseisle includes a biomass plant that generates more than 80 per cent of its annual demand of 10.2MW and pumps its waste hot water to the maltings on the site. The wood-pellet boiler at Aberfeldy cost £5 million, and even an apparently simple change – using a bigger proportion of recycled material in its gift cartons – involved Edrington Group and its suppliers in two whole years of research and experiment. So what's driving the industry to invest so heavily in becoming leaner and greener?

The obvious answer is that it all saves money; sadly, though, while the big corporations have made great environmental strides the new-wave small artisanal distillers have found themselves lagging behind. The reason is simple: cost. As one Scottish artisan distiller put it: 'We do what we can to reuse materials. Our draff [the malted barley residue that is left after the mashing process] goes to wild boar on a nearby farm and our pot ale is spread on the fields. But a big distillery can spend £400,000 to recover heat loss and even if it's only 10 per cent effective they'll still save a million; while for a small company like ours the heat loss equipment wouldn't save us anything. The long and the short of it is that you have to be a medium-sized distillery for this kind of equipment to be viable. Our kerosene boiler cost £28,000. The equivalent biomass plant would have cost £140,000.'

It's early days, though. English distillers are straining every sinew to answer, as it were, the call of nature; or rather, perhaps, it's the call of the wild. Technological innovations around sustainability have have entered the mainstream, reducing the expense of planning it into new-builds. Most English distillers are now able to incorporate environmental measures into their businesses from day one. For instance, here's how one unusually environmentally conscious distiller, Yorkshire's Cooper King, has tackled the issue:

- England's first net zero energy whisky is the result of six years' dedication to sustainability, including carbon footprint reduction, and is 27 years ahead of the government's 2050 net zero target.
- Cooper King donates £5 from the sale of every bottle of whisky to the Yorkshire Dales Millennium Trust to fund one apprentice each year through its rural apprenticeship scheme.
- Cooper King is one of only a handful of distilleries to have run on 100 per cent renewable energy from day one. This has hugely reduced the environmental impact of its operations, supports Britain's energy independence, and reduces reliance on fossil fuels. The maturation warehouse is ventilated by a solar-powered system and plans are underway to cover the distillery's entire roof with solar panels, which are expected to meet 75 per cent of its energy needs.
- Cooper King spirits carry the 1% For The Planet logo on their neck tag and labels, the first in Europe to do so. 1% For The Planet is an organisation that pairs environmentally minded businesses with environmental charities. Cooper King formally pledge to donate at least 1 per cent of all sales to the Yorkshire Dales Millennium Trust to spend on planting native woodland, restoring wildflower meadows and funding rural apprenticeships.
- Cooper King has achieved a 21 per cent reduction in energy and water use by using an insulating paint developed for NASA and by capturing and recycling hot water from the distillation process.
- The wooden stoppers in Cooper King bottles are made with a shank produced from an innovative material combining bio-based materials derived from sugar cane. It's co-injected into the wooden head, which means it is almost unbreakable and requires no glue. The tamper-proof seals used on the bottles are made from sustainably sourced wood cellulose rather than plastic and will biodegrade in your home compost in weeks.

CHAPTER FOUR

KIT & CABOODLE

INSIDE THE DISTILLERY

'Copper is not just a pretty metal: it's almost alive. Like an old forest tree it turns a peaceful green with age and exposure; yet its every atom fizzes with energy.'

The still house at Spirit of Yorkshire distillery.

One of the big attractions of distillery tours is that distilleries are beautiful. That's not the main attraction, of course: the main attraction is the tasting session at the end. But before you attain your nirvana, your pilgrimage will lead you through the stillroom and its copper-lined avenue of gleaming domes and spires. Well at least, the tour guide will point out a big shiny copper onion and a smaller shiny copper onion, each with a tall bent-double chimney also of shiny copper, that together dominate the old cowshed or other makeshift barn conversion you are standing in. These are the wash still and the spirit still, through which a vapour of rough strong beer will pass en route to becoming whisky. You will know if these vessels are actually at work or not because if they are, the cowshed/barn conversion will be bearably warm. If they're not, that means that the brewhouse will be busily preparing the wash for them to work on. Let's start there.

IS PURE WATER IMPORTANT?

When I worked for the Campaign for Real Ale, I proposed that water coolers should be dotted around the floor of the Great British Beer Festival so that attenders could rinse out their glasses without having to take them into the loo but more importantly, so that they could hydrate regularly between drinks in line with government health advice. To add a point of interest, I suggested that the water itself should be drawn from brewery boreholes, with their wells of origin prominently flagged. Then a representative of Charles Wells of Bedford, whose brewery has moved more than once but which has always been supplied from its original borehole, stopped my foolish mouth by reminding me of what I should have already known: that brewing liquor is generally so laden with salts and other necessary minerals that it is undrinkably foul. No festival goer would have thanked me had my suggestion been adopted!

The same is true of the water of which whisky is made. Greg Millar of Dartmoor Distillery in Bovey Tracy, Devon, trumpets the purity of the granite-filtered moorland water he uses for bottling. It's supplied by a specialist water company, Pure Dartmoor, which draws fresh water every day and as well as bottling it for retailers, it can analyse and guarantee for bulk customers like Greg. But he gets his wash from Princetown Brewery right up in the middle of the moor, and the brewing liquor they use up there must surely be equally pure...

mustn't it? Well, not necessarily. The main requirement of brewing liquor is that its mineral content must aid extraction during mashing and stimulate the yeast during fermentation; and the requisite minerals taste, as my friend at Charles Wells said, vile.

The brewing process neutralises the vile off-flavours and, as Greg pointed out, distillation does the same but more so. But where purity really does matter is in liquoring down the whisky after maturation. His whisky is bottled at 46 per cent abv, so 54 per cent of it is water – and the water is not from the tap but from Pure Dartmoor, which is the purest he can find. Others are equally picky: when the spring at Malvern, once bottled under its own name as the poshest water in the land, went out of business Dan Szor, the Cotswolds Distillery man, was on hand to snap it up. Water courses in many parts of Scotland will have picked up desirable flavours, especially smoke, if they run through peat bogs. But apart from diluting the cask-strength whisky and rendering it drinkable, the only effect he wants his water to produce is this: none.

EVOLUTION OF THE WASH

All spirits start life as fermented liquor of one sort or another – of wine or wine lees, of cider or perry, of palm-sap toddy, of molasses – and many craft distillers started life as producers of one or another of them. Indeed, the craft distilling movement started, because two cidermakers [Mssrs Bulmers and Temperley] foresaw an afterlife in the spirit world for their fermented liquors. In the case of whisky, the precursor liquor is unhopped beer known as wash and generally fermented to around 8–9 per cent abv. In the uncertain early days, before the Customs authorities became more user-friendly, both Hicks & Healey and Penderyn bought in their wash from neighbouring breweries – St Austell and Brain's respectively. As we have seen, HMRC has now conceded that whisky distilleries may brew their own wash, using kit that is both simple and, thanks to the market in suitably sized new and used vessels created by half a century of micro-brewing and craft brewing, generally affordable. It's not compulsory, of course, and many artisan distillers have neither the time nor the space for a full-blown brewery of their own – an exigency, which has led to many profitable and educational relationships between craft distillers and microbrewers.

The distillery brewhouse is effectively an everyday brewery, with a mashtun in which the grist is steeped and a washback where the resulting wort is fermented. What's missing, of course, is the copper where wort and hops are boiled together; what's also missing, therefore, is the flavour of hops in the finished wash, which is a liquid we laymen rarely think about. It's important to remember that though wash may be made of the same ingredients and broadly similar processes as ale – i.e. unhopped beer – it isn't ale. I have already mentioned Brother John Cor and his bolls of malt for making *aquae vitae*, but there's no way of knowing whether the liquor he intended for the still was the same unhopped ale that he and his brethren enjoyed every day; but today – well, a pint of wash wouldn't be so enjoyable. For just as cognac is distilled from weak, acidic wines you certainly wouldn't want to drink, so malt whiskies derive from ales so well-attenuated that even tasting them is more of a chore than a pleasure. One craft distiller describes the wash from which his whisky is created as 'thin and weedy', explaining that what he wants for a pure and untainted spirit is as thorough a conversion of the mash as possible, achieving a thin and frankly sour wash of 9–10 per cent abv with a final gravity right down at 1000°. The wash in this case is pretty much at the top of the range in terms of alcohol content: at the bottom comes Adnams's Copper House distillery, which uses unhopped Broadside at 6.7 per cent abv as the wash for its eau-de-vie de bière, conceived one day when the team was in playful mood and found to be 'unusual, but good'.

Outbreaks of playfulness may crop up regularly among micro-brewers and gin rectifiers, where complete ruin is unlikely to follow the spoliation of a single batch. But as Copper House's John McCarthy told the Master of Malt online merchant's blog: 'With our grain to glass approach, the brewers had to learn to make a distillery wash. There are differences. When you brew beer, you want (the mash) to be at a certain temperature so you get a make-up of sugars that are fermentable and non-fermentable. You want long chain sugars like dextrin, because you want sweetness. And you want sugars that are smaller, like maltose and glucose, which will ferment into alcohol. You want alcohol, but you also need to retain some sugars that will not ferment. That's beer. When you make a distillery wash, you want it all to be fermentable because you can't distil sugar.

The sour, anorexic character of so many washes is also down to the yeast most distillers use these days. The modern strain was developed about 60 years ago to work fast, to ferment every last grain of sugar, and to survive the heat and alcohol it itself generates. More recently its environmental benefits, particularly its reduced water and energy inputs, have gained in prominence and esteem, and only a handful of distillers still use old-school brewer's yeasts. But despite the cutting-edge biochemistry, whisky distillers still use some ancient techniques. Just like a medieval alewife, most mash their malt three times, getting progressively weaker worts. These worts are usually blended before fermentation, but practices vary: at Glenfarclas, for instance, the weak wort from the third mash becomes the liquor for the first mash of the next batch.

An equally ancient practice that has recently made a comeback, albeit on a tiny scale, explains the story of the drunken duck, which owed its inebriation to an accident that would be largely impossible today. The brewer threw out the spent grains; the duck naturally gobbled them up. As they were still saturated in beer the duck got plastered with (of course) hilarious consequences. This is only possible if you ferment your wort without running it off your grain (or 'goods'); which might have been common practice when the duck got drunk, but certainly isn't today.

MACERATION

The experimental distillers Frances Oates and John Clotworthy of Loch Ewe in Wester Ross, now retired, took speed and efficiency of fermentation to an extreme. During their historical research they discovered that many bothiemen fermented their wash by maceration – that is, without troubling to strain it off the grist, as above, but only giving it time to cool a little before pitching it with yeast. The enhanced contact between yeast and malt allowed the friendly fungus to keep on working right up to its natural limit of 18–20 per cent alcohol by volume, twice the abv to which washes are generally fermented today, at which point the highly toxic CO_2 and alcohol colluded in the murder of their parent.

This high-contact fermentation was not only fast: it was also so violent that it gave off a palpable warmth that must have been very welcome to the bothieman and, of course, his obligatory boy and their dog in their makeshift still house out on the moor. The resulting wash with its higher starting volume could be rushed through the two stages of distillation, racked into small casks and loaded on to the pack ponies in two shakes of a Shetland's tail, which was of course the whole point of all the haste in the first place. The less time they took, the less risk they ran of detection. The diminutive pony-portable casks also prolonged the contact time between oak and spirit, hastening maturation.

I do not know of any other British whisky distillers who follow where Frances and John led: there would certainly be a danger of producing something quite undrinkable, which the Loch Ewe two avoided by selling all their product as new make rather than finished whisky as, they said, the bothiemen used to do. For the legitimate distillers of the sixteenth and seventeenth centuries, as we have seen, maturation was the entire economic *raison d'être* whereas for the hunted smuggler of the eighteenth century it was up to the customer to risk keeping a cellarful of dodgy casks and take their chances with the excise.

But eccentric as maceration may seem in the context of modern whisky, it is a method of fermentation still common in other regions of the global drinks industry: in the American distilling industry, for instance, and wherever they make red wine.

'A lot of Bourbon distillers still do it this way and it produces fantastic results,' John once told me. 'With the malt still in the wort the yeast can digest all the sugar, and we get low wines that aren't 18–25 per cent abv but 45–50 per cent!' Not to mention a fermentation so hot that on a cold day you can warm your hands on it.

More recently an opposite approach is being tried. Brewers describe a week-long fermentation as being 'blessed by the Sabbath' because the wort must, mathematically, spend at least one Sunday in the fermenter. A slower, cooler fermentation brings out the fruitier flavours. It's a technique used by Dariusz Plazewski of London's Bimber distillery; and in Bimber's case the effect is enhanced by the use of a self-built American oak washback.

WASH AND SPIRIT STILLS

It is not, however, the brewhouse we have come to see, no matter how fascinating and how idiosyncratic it might be. It's the copper, the gleaming copper in all its shining beauty and with all its promise of drams to come that lures us and holds us.

Copper is not just a pretty metal: it's almost alive. Like an old forest tree it turns a peaceful green with age and exposure; yet its every atom fizzes with energy when it guards your house from lightning or carries your voice to a loved one far away. For copper loves us and wants us to be happy. You can tell that it loves us by the way it bends to every tap of the raising hammer and parts at the merest kiss of the tinsnips, and by the obliging way it transmutes the sulphides in the liquor that can taint the spirit, turning them into sulphates that pelletise and either sink harmlessly or cling to the sides of the still, to be cleaned off with a wipe of lemon juice.

Perhaps it's an effect of copper's allure that makes us think of distillation as the science of separating liquids of different densities by evaporation. In truth, it might be better defined as the science of separating liquids of different densities by condensation, since it's not all that difficult to light a fire under a bucket of wash but damned tricky to recapture only the vapours one actually wants. The condenser is a subject to which we shall return, but first let's get the wash vaporised, which requires us to dwell a little longer on the subject of copper.

THE COPPER REVOLUTION

Copper has a mightier story than we might today imagine. It was known and exploited from prehistoric times mostly, since its deposits were often coterminous with those of the tin (as in Devon and Cornwall) with which it was fused in the production of hard, sharp, workable bronze. Its readiness to meld with other metals made copper the bridge on which humankind crossed the chasm between ancient and modern. That was countless generations ago, and between that era and this copper was eclipsed by iron in almost every use except bell-founding. But in the fourteenth century AD gunpowder arrived from the Orient. Now Mars met Euterpe; war met music; and a great love-match it proved to be. The demands of war were satisfied by the provision of music, both bells and guns being up to 90 per cent copper and gun-casting and bell-founding being near-identical crafts. Prelate and prince alike craved copper in measure that could never be requited, the one to magnify the Lord, the other to betray Him. Throughout the fourteenth and fifteenth centuries, therefore, new deposits were sought, and being sought, were found. A huge worldwide metallurgical industry grew on these foundations, with parties of prospectors being sponsored by imperial and royal promoters to found new mines as far apart as Potosi and Kendal. Gold and silver ignited the lust of the powerful, but copper, tin and lead proved in their humdrum way just as able to slake it. The more familiar Industrial Revolution in the early nineteenth century might be characterised as humankind's discovery of energy – of gravity and water, of coal and coke, of their gases, and, most gloriously, of electricity; none of it would have happened if mankind had not mastered precious metals 300 years before.

Inside the still house at Spirit of Yorkshire Distillery.

The availability of copper, the evolution of a Europe-wide corps of coppersmiths to work it, and the metal's own malleability and durability, persuaded apothecaries and infirmarers to throw out their table-top retorts of glass and earthenware and invest instead – just as we saw Henry VI's Master of Stillatories doing in the mid-fifteenth century – in much larger, much cheaper and much more hard-wearing copper replacements. And in humbler homes the copper pots intended for brewing and laundry proved adaptable to make perfectly practical if rough-and-ready stills. Earlier we attributed the rise of spirit production to the discovery that malt liquor could be distilled just as successfully as wine, and for a fraction of the cost. Now we need to acknowledge that copper was an equal partner in the parentage of whisky.

DIFFERENT STILLS

There are, practically, two kinds of still in widespread commercial use: the pot still, which will process one batch of liquor at a time, and the column or continuous still which, as its name suggests, operates continuously. There are also vacuum stills, which employ pressure differentials rather than temperature differentials to separate liquids

of different densities. They are often touted as more economical to run than heat-operated stills, but in fact it takes as much energy to run a vacuum pump as it does to heat a conventional still, and a vacuum still is much more prone to leaks. Broadly speaking, then (very broadly speaking, actually) the finer malt whiskies and cognacs are produced in batches in pot stills while purer but less characterful spirits such as grain whisky and the ethanol you might use as the foundation of your gin come from column stills.

THE POT STILL

The pot still seems to have been invented in the eighth or ninth century AD by Arabian chemists in Baghdad, principally as a bench-top retort on which to produce solvents for the manufacture of medicines, lacquers and cosmetics. It had spread to Christendom via the great cosmopolitan medical school at Salerno by the late eleventh century, but the spirits it produced were still used almost entirely as industrial and medical solvents until the fifteenth century.

The two-part copper stills that originated in the later Middle Ages had huge advantages over the simple glass or earthenware laboratory retorts and condensers hitherto used by apothecaries, alchemists and infirmarers. One was that they could make much greater volumes in the larger vessels made from sheet metal than ones made from glass or pottery; the other was that changing the shape of the head, allowed distillers to experiment with different condensation temperatures and thereby learn to manipulate the chemical composition of the eventual spirit. Big fat necks with large surface areas, they discovered, changed sulphites into sulphates as we have noted, but also cooled quickly enough to separate out such impurities as they condense at lower temperatures than ethanol, leaving a smoother (as well as a safer) spirit. Similarly, tall necks cooled toward the top, causing some of the vapour to condense and trickle back down into the still, to vaporise again after shedding some of the harsher, oilier compounds and thus produce a lighter spirit.

Through long trial and error distillers all over Christendom learned what they and their customers wanted; and over a period of more than four centuries pot-still shapes and configurations evolved by rule of thumb. Apart from modifications to their dimensions, the only major changes since then have been in the method of heating them, from wooden or charcoal direct fires, to coke and coal-heated steam coils, to gas-fired coils. Reliable industrial thermometers weren't available until the 1750s, and even then were slow to catch on. Given that a still is at bottom a heat-exchanger in which considerations such as the total surface area and thickness of the metal, the temperature within the still and the ambient temperature outside it are crucial, this makes it all the more miraculous that any potable spirit was produced at all. Even today, while the principles are well understood, the variables are so many and complex that predicting how an individual still will perform and what it will produce is as much a matter of experience and intuition as of science.

All pot-distilled spirit, just about, goes through two distillations. The wash still produces 'low wines' of about 20–30 per cent abv, leaving impurities including aldehydes and congeners behind. The spirit still is generally somewhat smaller than its precursor; a single pass through it refines the low wines to a legally permitted maximum concentration of 94.8 per cent abv – close to the azeotrope (a mixture of two liquids which has a constant boiling point and composition throughout distillation). But in practice much closer to 70 per cent. Some distilleries pass this new make through the spirit still once more for luck; but the real magic doesn't happen in the stills at all. It's what happens next that's the clever bit.

Inside the still house at The Lakes Distillery.

THE COLUMN OR CONTINUOUS STILL

The continuous still in which mixed-grain whisky and pure ethanol are made is an ingenious example of thermodynamic engineering and dates from the 1820s. A number of pioneering variants were designed and built of which one, a modification of an original patented by an Irish distiller named Perrier in 1822, found favour with big lowland distillers seeking to produce pure spirit for the English gin market. But the first to produce and patent a design suitable for the whisky industry was an Irish excise officer, Aeneas Coffey, in 1830.

The Coffey still had and indeed has many advantages over the traditional pot. For a start, given a basic minimum of diastatic barley-malt in its grist, it could distil a wash made of any old grain including wheat, rye, oats, sugar-rich maize and even cereals contaminated at sea, damaged in warehouse fires and floods, sodden by storms, hit by lightning, attacked by rats and weevils, tainted by the malice of Cthulhu or anything else.

Its production efficiency, though, was its principal attraction. A pot stills processes a batch at a time. A continuous still – hence the name – simply doesn't stop. It and its modern descendants comprise

Inside the still house at Spirit of Yorkshire distillery. On the right is a pot still and behind the operator is a four plate rectifying column still that works in tandem with the spirit pot still. This allows them to produce two different styles of new make spirit.

two columns of copper, the analyser and the rectifier. A continuous stream of wash, entering at ambient temperature, circulates through the rectifier and into the analyser, where it encounters a blast of steam. The steam evaporates the alcohol out of the wash, and the whole cloud of mixed vapours rises to a funnel through which it is piped into the rectifier to be separated into its component parts by the cooling effect of the ambient wash. Yes, folks: the continuous still recycles its own heat. The wash, fresh and cool from the fermenting vessel, warms up while the steam, through contact with the wash, condenses at different temperatures into its constituent liquids, which are collected on plates and drained off separately as they do so. One of these separated liquids is ethanol, which is collected at 95.63 per cent pure. This is the azeotrope, the point at which further boiling will not remove any more of the water. To me, the continuous still is like watching a really good stage magician. I know what's being done; I might even have a vague idea of how. But I'm at a complete loss to explain it to anyone else. However, as continuous distillation is not really part of the artisan whisky distiller's armoury, it's not so important.

THE iSTILL

In the iStill, patented in 2012 in Holland, the future meets the past in a way that could well transform the economics and hence the fortunes of artisan distilling. This new form of still is not as conceptually revolutionary as the continuous still was when it came out 200 years ago: it's the offspring of crossing different technologies rather than creating an entirely new one. But its operational potential is unfathomable.

At bottom, what we have here is a neat and tidy version of the computerised control of processes and vessels that the brewing industry has been accustomed to for years. If you had been shown around a major brewery in the 1970s and '80s it would have been teeming with blokes in overalls and steelies, all of them looking very busy at some occupation or other whose nature and function were utterly ineffable. On the same tour in the '90s you would have been shown a single enormous console served by one or at most two collared-and-tied acolytes, quite possibly with degrees. Anyone else you saw hanging about would have been an electrician with not a great deal to do.

So it is with the iStill. We're not going to go into too much detail here because this is primarily a book for gawpers, not technicians; and besides, the iStill is more a triumph of design than of pure innovation. The most obvious difference is that the iStill is cubical rather than columnar or domed – something to do, I believe, with improving the thermodynamic convection and (possibly) the even distribution of all the groogly bits. Inside the box is a single stainless steel vessel (although a copper variant is available) in which all the processes are conducted, so that not only fermentation but also distillation take place on the grist, with consequent advantages in extraction. The copper contact can be supplied by the use of looms of copper thread, although the standard model comes fitted with mats of small steel coils; reflux is controlled by a neck that rises and falls; the plates in the column are, again, woven looms of copper or steel wire, and the cuts are pre-programmed to be made at exactly the same point every time.

And all this is controlled by a programme of your own specification, so that you can turn it all on and fall asleep or operate it remotely from your sales trip to Tegucigalpa using the app on your iPhone. The sorcerer no longer needs an apprentice; the brew will always be true; energy use will be cut by 200 per cent (I'm not quite sure what that means, but it is undoubtedly highly beneficial). An entire distillery, then, costing very little to buy and install, and very little to run, which can be operated by anyone with the most meagre of IT skills. There'll be a distillery on every street corner at this rate, you just see if there isn't.

SOURCING STILLS

A persistent challenge for artisan distillers in England has been to source a workable and affordable still. One difference between the early days of the microbrewing boom and the current artisan distilling revival is that small breweries were much cheaper and easier to equip. Not only could a skilled – or even, in some cases, a semi-skilled – fabricator cobble up a perfectly serviceable brewery from more or less any old vessels, but the failure rate in the early days was such that there was always plenty of second-hand kit floating about. Distilling equipment, on the other hand, is less easy to improvise. And although the first two English craft distilleries, King Offa and Somerset Royal, were kitted out with virtually antique alembics ambulants or mobile stills sourced, appropriately enough, in Calvados country, there is far less second-hand distilling equipment on the market than there is brewing equipment. That means buying new – but where?

The British distilling industry is highly specialised and until recently has been very stable both in terms of the number of operators shopping for new equipment and of the kind of equipment they require. For the most part the established whisky and gin distillers have needed big vessels either to replace the old ones they already have or to equip the vast new super-distilleries they are frenziedly constructing. They also have long lead-in times: it's possible to predict when an elderly still will need replacing some years in advance, while the equipment for a big new plant can more or less be ordered off-plan and fabricated while the distillery buildings themselves are going up. In short, the market for new distilling equipment has until now been dominated by demand for big, costly, custom-built kit. By the same token, the discarded equipment put up for sale has tended to consist of large and expensive units. Not very helpful for the would-be craft distiller – although do have a sneaky look at the distilling and brewing page on www.perryprocess.co.uk, because you never know what you'll find!

Having said all that, there's no reason why you shouldn't build your distillery from scratch – plenty have. Provided you're a competent engineer you can source all the tankage, pipework, pumps, heat exchangers, cip (cleaning in place) attachment and so forth that you need from the UK microbrewing supply industry. You can also commission a perfectly good still from any competent fabricator with a proven record of making robust pressure-proof vessels. I only know of one example, that of Tadweld, an established supplier of vessels to the drinks industry in the Yorkshire brewing centre of Tadcaster, which fabricated a still for Whittaker's; but there is no earthly reason why other boilermakers (as they used to be known) should not pitch for the business. Meanwhile, most distillers are looking across the Channel for their hardware. All over Europe, wherever there's a vineyard or a cider mill or a brewery, there's a distillery somewhere close by; and wherever there's a distillery there's a coppersmith manufacturing and maintaining its array of vessels. English distillers have taken trips to Galicia to browse the Hoga catalogue (www.hogacompany.com); to Italy to check out Metalox (www.barisantechgroup.en.ec21.com); to Portugal for a tour of Iberian Coppers (www.copper-alembic. com); to Bordeaux to sample the claret but with a detour to Bègles on the outskirts of the city to look in at the third-generation family firm Alambics Stupfler.

All these companies – and dozens like them all over Belgium, the Netherlands, Scandinavia, Germany, Austria, Switzerland, Croatia, Czechia, Slovakia, Poland and just about everywhere else where a tradition of small-scale distilling has survived – fabricate solid, high-quality, hand-crafted pot stills, columns, condensers and other equipment including barrels perfectly suited to the English artisan distiller.

THE CONDENSER

It took the first alchemists a few generations to learn how to recondense the vapours they had created. For if you see distillation not so much as a process of creating desirable flavours as one of stripping out the undesirable ones, then it's not the business of boiling it all up that really matters but the business of cooling it all down in steps that can be separated. All the various component compounds vaporise and condense at different temperatures. The key ones are 78.4^0C, which is the boiling/condensation point of ethanol, and 64.7^0C, which is the boiling/condensation point of its evil twin methanol – you know, the one that metabolises as formic acid and makes you blind.

Condensers have taken many forms over the years. Medieval apothecaries and infirmarers used coiled glass tubes, cooled with running water: efficient enough, no doubt, but tricky to make and very fragile. Some of the earliest farm-based whisky distillers appear to have dangled a loosely rolled sheepskin over the still and when it was well-sodden hung it over a barrel to drip. The ancient Chinese and Mongolians had an effective alternative, a version of which is still widely used at sea to collect brine desalinated by solar power. To visualise the ancient Oriental still, imagine a three-tier openwork gantry standing over a low fire. On the lowest tier is a wide shallow bowl containing the liquor to be distilled. On the next tier up is a much narrower bowl or even a beaker; while on the top is an inverted cone made of copper and filled with cold water or, even better, ice. The fire is just hot enough to evaporate the alcohol from the wine. The vapour condenses on the cold underside of the cone, runs down it and drips into the beaker (or, I suppose, spirit receiver). You can immediately see the problem with this set-up: the condenser collects all the alcohols from the wine indiscriminately – those you want and those you don't; those that are wholesome, and those that will eventually kill you. The spirit might be perfectly suitable as a solvent for cosmetics, but not so good as a neutral base for beverages!

The marine solar still commonly kept in a yachtsman's emergency grab bag works on a very similar principle. It consists of a transparent plastic bowl very like a life preserver, with a cone, again of transparent plastic, mounted on top of it but the other way up. The shipwrecked mariner fills the bowl with seawater and seals up the cone. The sun – assuming our yachtsman has turned turtle in the Tropics – evaporates the brine and the steam condenses on the inner surface of the cone into droplets of clean water. These trickle down into a gutter mounted around the circumference where bowl and cone join, and thence into a reservoir. This device will work either on the raft or (provided it isn't too rough) floating in the sea. But for obvious reasons, do tie it to your wrist or ankle before committing it to the waves!

These makeshifts may have been practical enough but given the cheapness of copper in the sixteenth and seventeenth centuries and the skill of the coppersmiths of the time, a metal version of the alchemist's wormtub was quickly adopted as the universal condenser. After the introduction of excise in the 1640s the curly pipe was the only dead giveaway that a jumble of copper buckets and other bits and pieces was indeed a distillery rather than a brewery. But its utility was such that it remained irreplaceable, and there are working examples still to be seen – if seeing a coiled copper tune is your bag, that is – to this very day.

The spirit safe at Spirit of Yorkshire Distillery.

THE SPIRIT SAFE

The spirit-safe is the item of unobtrusive but essential kit you'd walk straight past if someone who knew what it was didn't tell you. Basically, it's not much more than a viewing panel set into the outlet from condenser to receiver, with a switching system that allows the flow to be redirected as appropriate.

The whole distilling process is, as far as possible, a closed system that ringfences HMRC's revenues. A distillery has by law to be completely secure, not so much from the natural tendencies of the criminal underworld as from the incurable cupidity of distillery workers and owners. Not only must the former be prevented from scrumping a bit here and there to take home, but the latter must be deterred from diverting even more substantial quantities in order to escape duty. But the stillman has to be able to intervene to take off the heads and tails and allowing only the middle cut or heart to take to its oaken bed for a long and lonely sleep of maturation. Access to the spirit itself is barred by a large and sometimes decorative padlock whose key, until 1983, was kept by the local customs officer. Distillery managers now have a key too, but woe betide them if they use it!

PROOF IF PROOF WERE NEEDED

No alcohol is entirely pure. It has an azeotrope of 95.63 per cent ethanol by volume to 4.37 per cent water, beyond which it cannot be made any purer by conventional distillation because it has a boiling point lower than either of its components. From the moment the science of distillation crossed the Mediterranean from Tunisia, brought perhaps by Constantine the African to the Medical School at Salerno in about 1065, it was important to be able to gauge the purity of the spirit in order to make it the basis of safe and reliable medicines. One early test of purity, transcribed in 1351 in *Das Water des Levens op Levende Water* by Jan Van Aalter from an earlier but now lost Flemish original, involved periodically dipping a burning cloth or wick into the spirit receiver as it slowly filled up. Once the liquid was weak enough to extinguish the flame the distillation had reached the 'tails', composed of less volatile alcohols such as propanol and butanol, carbohydrates, proteins and water, which were then collected separately for redistillation. This test did not measure the alcoholic strength – a concept unknown to those who applied it – and neither did it detect the far more toxic foreshots, the first 5 per cent of distillate composed mainly of methanol, which was not isolated until 1661; but then the drams of physic prescribed to late medieval and early modern patients were too meagre to cause a toxic accumulation of the formic acid that is methanol's metabolite – and probably insufficient to do much good either.

But once spirits had evolved beyond their original *raison d'être* as physic to a much wider use as beverage, and consumers started using them in much greater quantities, they attracted the attention of the taxation authorities in many Dutch and German cities, and various methods of measuring not the alcohol content but the water content were devised, many of which not unnaturally involved fire. According to Professor Eric van Schoonenberghe of the Hasselt Genever Museum in Belgium: 'Until the seventeenth century there were several ways to determine the alcohol content. A brandy had only been rightly distilled if it completely burned without leaving any humidity behind, an oil drop sank in it, a drop of it put on a hand evaporated entirely, a bucket filled with it completely burned up, or camphor melted in it.'

THE GUNPOWDER METHOD

The method best-known to us today, perhaps because it seems the most arcane, was the gunpowder test. Alcohol had already played a part in the development of gunpowder when manufacturers discovered its superiority over water in moistening the ground-up saltpetre, carbon and sulphur before mixing: it leached some of the potassium out of the saltpetre and made the resulting powder more inflammable. Now gunpowder was returning the favour. 'A spoonful of gunpowder was showered with brandy and held in a burning candle,' says van Schoonenberghe. 'If the brandy contained too much water, the gunpowder would not catch fire.' The ratio necessary for the test or proof to succeed was 57.15 per cent alcohol to 42.85 per cent water; 57.15 per cent was therefore declared, in an age before percentages were common currency, 100° proof. The origin of this test appears to have lain with the British navy at some time in the late sixteenth century, and it was nothing to do with tax as some have suggested because excise (from the Dutch *accijs*, tellingly enough) wasn't levied on liquor in Britain until 1643.

It seems in fact to have been related to naval gunnery. In rough weather, with sea-spray flying everywhere, linstocks and matches were commonly waterproofed with a paste of spirit and gunpowder, which wouldn't remain alight if the spirit were too watery, as above. This is an explanation that begs a few questions, and only a practical experiment would validate it; but in any case the Dutch had a far more practical method of determining proof, which was universally adopted by British distillers for day-to-day use. They half-filled a glass vial with the spirit to be tested, sealed it and gave it a vigorous shake. The denser the liquid – i.e., the more water it contained, since spirit is lighter than water – the more slowly the bubbles would disperse. At proof, a foamy head would form. Proof in the UK today is still counted as 57.15 per cent abv; in the US, and with no slow-matches and linstocks to be kept aglow, it's a more convenient 50 per cent. The *Hollandse proef* or Dutch test was accepted all over Europe and would only be generally supplanted in the nineteenth century when the hydrometer (used since the seventeenth century for assaying coins) became a standard piece of brewery and distillery equipment.

CHAPTER FIVE

OAK & AGEING

PUSHING THE BOUNDARIES

'Most English whisky distillers – although not quite all – relish the opportunity for innovation, diversity and creativity that comes from the imaginative use of refill casks.'

Whisky casks at The Lakes Distillery.

Oak is magical stuff, and not just to Druids. It's as prominent in the story of alcohol as the grape and the grain themselves, and it was time spent in oak that set proto-gin and proto-whisky on their divergent courses.

The first thing to note is that in the late sixteenth century when (according to me) whisky started to become whisky, oak barrels were everywhere, universally used for storing and transporting every commodity from butter to pickled herring. And ale, of course. They were an expensive form of packaging, true; but they were marvellously durable, infinitely refillable, and since they contained not a single nail, let alone a screw, easily repairable. And when every village had its coopers and oak trees dominated the forest, they were ubiquitous.

Coopers used other timber as well as oak, of course: chestnut was also popular. But oak had peculiar properties that made it the tree of choice. In its green state it was soft enough to work; and although it hardened as it dried it remained porous, so that its capillaries could be made to swell up and hold the bevelled staves together more firmly than any glue then known. Its straight grain meant that when still green it was easy to split into long strakes using only axe and wedge – the axe's blade splitting the trunk open, the flat face driving in the wedges until a rough plank came away to be shaped and planed. Less need for a sawpit then, nor for a hand-cut saw blade that dulled every few minutes, nor for the eyes and lungs of the bottom sawyer to be constantly full of sawdust.

Green oak's soft springiness also made possible one of the most practical and beautiful design features in the entire history of engineering: the bilge. Simply by tapering the fresh-cut staves so that the finished cask would have a fat waist, the cooper transformed a cylinder which could only be rolled back and forth into a barrow that supported its own weight, turned on its own axis, and could be tilted laterally to squeeze through a narrow opening. Manoeuvrability, thy name is barrel! But there's more. The bilge also meant that a barrel wouldn't slip out of hoists or slings where they were used – on a quay, especially; and it acted as a trap for ullage – the 'tilts' that early distillers were encouraged to make full use of.

Holding the whole thing together, the traditional hoops would also be a delight to the modern conservationist. Before the Industrial Revolution when iron bands became so cheap and easy to fabricate

Inside a warehouse at The Lakes Distillery where they use ex-bourbon casks and sherry butts.

that it would have seemed criminal not to use them, barrel-hoops were simply rings of plaited withy. Soaked and swollen before being put on, hammered down and allowed to dry, their natural elasticity shrank them back to their original shape and size and gave them the grip of a pit-bull terrier – and not just a mildly annoyed one, either. Looked at as a whole, the humble old-style oak barrel is Greta Thunberg's dream packaging: clean, green, reusable, biodegradable and almost as strong as Greta herself.

THE BIG BOTANICAL

Forest trees possess natural defences against pests and predators – for instance, there's nothing more effective than a cedar lining to keep the moths out of your knicker drawer, while in the 1960s and beyond pine resin was the universal scent of Britain's kitchens. Oak is no exception. The acidic antioxidant tannin in which all parts of the plant are so rich is poison to most bacteria, fungi and livestock (except pigs, which will happily rootle on acorns all autumn long – and with every tree bearing up to 90,000 acorns, they'll still leave plenty for the squirrels) and thereby helps to preserve whisky over long years of maturation. Over time, tannin also metabolises aldehydes, neutralising their harsh bitterness. Vanillin, naturally present in oak, is another effective insecticide, which has been used for centuries and perhaps millennia to repel bedbugs, mosquitoes, fleas and other biting insects. Being bloodsuckers, it seems they find the warm vanilla aroma we so cherish just too sickly for their taste. These and other aromatic preservatives present in oak, then, have exactly the same effect as the botanicals in gin, only instead of steeping or steaming the botanicals in the spirit, you seal the spirit into a vessel that incorporates the botanicals.

CHARRED REMAINS

Like a really good steak, an oak barrel benefits enormously from being broiled briefly but at a very high temperature. Nobody really knows when, where or why the process originated; but it seems a fair bet that when barrels were the universal trade container, pretty drastic measures were required between fills to get rid of the aroma of pickled herring. The traditional method of cleaning the barrels' insides was to insert lengths of chain and detail the apprentices to roll the casks up and down the yard for an hour two – noisier than today's high-pressure steam, and a lot more energetic, but a bit of harmless fun for the youngsters. Probably not really up to pickled herrings, mind, hence the fire.

But charring the barrels does more than just incinerate the last trace of herring. Oak, as we have seen, is porous, but its surface is hard. Charring its insides with a gas-jet breaks the surface and allows the spirit to penetrate the wood, setting up interactions that add some characteristics and mask or filter out others (charcoal being one of the finest natural filters known to humanity). Clearly, then, the depth of char is critical to the barrel's performance in action. Typically, charring is divided into four levels or degrees of intensity. Level 1 exposes the staves to the gas-jet for 15–20 seconds, while at level 2 the torture lasts for 30–35 seconds. Barrels fired – or merely scorched, really – at these levels are referred to as 'toasted' and are rarely if ever used to mature the spirit but to finish it, bringing out the sweeter notes of coffee, caramel and vanilla. Maturation at levels 3 (35–40 seconds) and 4 (55–60 seconds) confers the deep, rich copper colour and caramel flavour favoured by the bourbon distillers on whom Scotland's supply of barrels largely depends (see below).

Naturally these gradations are elastic, and charring can be taken as deeply as the customer demands short of complete immolation. But firing at much more than level 4 – which dries, blackens and breaks the inner surfaces of the staves into a pattern of squares that look like an alligator's scaly skin – is a highly specialised requirement favoured by artisan distillers with a penchant for mould-breaking. Only this extreme charring creates the intense smokiness one finds in most Islay whiskies: it provides a peat-free alternative to achieving smokiness, although perhaps an admixture of Rauchmalz might do the same job less messily. Charring's principal effect, however, is to bring out the round notes, especially vanilla, and the various wood sugars that derive from chemical changes such as the breaking down of hemicellulose during charring.

BARRELS FROM THE USA

All these conventions and traditions, it should be noted, belong to the US, which furnishes British distilleries with most of our barrels and thereby determines, to a certain extent, what our distillers can and cannot do. This phenomenon stems ostensibly from 1935, when the Federal Alcohol Authority (FAA) was established to bring order to the chaos that followed the 1933 repeal of Prohibition. A large part of the FAA's remit was to stamp out the continuing bootlegging and

Bourbon barrels being charred at the Brown-Forman cooperage in Kentucky, USA.

counterfeiting carried on by mobsters who had done well out of Prohibition and didn't see any reason to stop. Even though whiskeys of various sorts were now legal, the mob's version – tax-free, of course; made in all probability of broken biscuits and old bus tickets; and finished with creosote – was still going to be a lot cheaper. One of the FAA's indispensable weapons against counterfeiting was to be a strict set of legal definitions against which bootleg products could be tested; and according to the excellent American website thewhiskeyjug.com: 'The most important part of this piece of legislation (was) the creation of even more specific definitions of what exactly constitutes a rye whiskey, bourbon etc, and also the requirement for new charred oak barrels to be used.'

There was, however, a double purpose in the new regulations. As well as a weapon against the mob, it was a badly needed job creation measure in the logging and coopering industries. As thewhiskeyjug. com goes on: 'There's a lot of discussion about who exactly got the new oak requirement passed through, but one of the more popular theories is that it stems from lobbying by the coopers' union as a means to secure jobs. It may have also had connections to the

Arkansas lumber industry. What's important is that it secured the use of new oak containers in the creation of certain types of whiskey.' The insertion of this clause, however it came about, was a godsend not only to the American lumberjacks and coopers whose jobs it secured but also to Scotch whisky distillers, whose supply of casks and kegs it also safeguarded. Throughout the nineteenth and early twentieth centuries Britain's consumption of oak for industrial and military purposes – as railway sleepers, pit-props, industrial buildings great and small, deck planking, beer barrels and even weather-resistant paving setts – grew exponentially while replanting lagged far behind. World War I made even heavier demands, and in 1919 the Forestry Commission was founded to regulate the UK's attempts at reforestation. It was fine for pine, but growing hardwood is a slow business that can't be hurried, and what replanting had been carried out from the 1890s could not even nearly meet the demands of the 1930s.

NEW MAKE IN OLD BARRELS

Coopers, those craftsmen par excellence who make and repair wooden barrels by hand and eye alone, used to be more or less ubiquitous in English towns and cities but have now died out south of the border, with just a handful still working in the few breweries, which still use oak barrels mainly, it has to be confessed, for display to the visitors. Another vanished source of second-hand barrels was the independent grocer. As late as the 1960s every high street had one or two; and many of them were wine merchants, too, with sticky barrels of sherry and port for apprentices to bottle by hand – and to share the proceeds of the inevitable pilfering with friends after work. After the bottling (and slurping) was done, the empties were flogged cheap to whoever could take them away. The yard at my own local independent, Addison's of Newport in Shropshire, was always crammed with barrels of wine awaiting bottling, tea chests awaiting decanting (indispensable packaging for the removal trade), and other imports including, oddly, a huge range of charcuterie; Addison's is still in business as a highly respected wine shipper and wholesaler, but is unlikely to ship its wares in barrels or tonneaux today. The wine shippers of the great port cities, such as Oporto, were a good source of second-hand barrels, too: rum casks imported into Bristol and Plymouth from the Caribbean were particularly favoured by the region's cidermakers.

A cooper at work in the Speyside Cooperage.

Gone, alas, all gone. But the near-extinction of coopers and used barrels in England is no problem, because Scotland is absolutely stuffed with them and the biggest, the French-owned Speyside Cooperage of Craigellachie, is part of a worldwide web of winemakers and can source pretty much anything a distiller wants to play with. Mongolian kvass-casks may be a bit thin on the ground, but if you've got the money...

Before the seemingly unlimited supply of charred American first fill bourbon barrels started to arrive in Britain, the industry, of course, made its own barrels both in the distilleries themselves and in the many independent cooperages that flourished; but second-hand was cheaper, and throughout the eighteenth century ex-sherry casks were the most popular – perhaps because they were the most

numerous. Other fortified wine casks were also widely used, as were cognac casks. Battered and patched as these barrels undoubtedly were after years of use and reuse, they could be made new easily enough by the distilleries' coopers. A few well-placed blows with chisel and maul freed the hoops and heads, and the staves could then either be planed clean or, if too worn, replaced entirely. But however thoroughly planed, these barrels never completely lost the character of their original contents, traces of which still lingered in the wood's capillaries. Since fortified wines, especially sherry and port but also Malmsey (a sweet wine from Madeira) and its many variants, were far, far more popular a century ago than they are now, whiskies matured in their casks (brandy and rum casks likewise) were inclined to the sweet, rich and heavy, while the predominating American white oak first-fills produce lighter, less extreme malts ideal for blending with the near-neutral product of the Coffey still.

But there's a problem. In the American distilling industry, pressure is growing for the prohibition on reuse to be at least relaxed if not scrapped altogether. American distillers protest that it piles on unnecessary overheads, and many go on to protest that it denies them the chance to experiment and innovate in the field of maturation. If they are successful and our supply of used barrels dries up, there will still be plenty of capacity in the US to supply British demand, and there is spare capacity across Europe, too. For now, though, there are more than enough single-use bourbon casks for first-fill maturation, as well as a staggering array of different wine fills to finish their malts in, increasing their ranges at a considerable price premium. Most English whisky distillers – although not quite all – relish the opportunity for innovation, diversity and creativity that comes from the imaginative use of refills. Indeed, one of Brittany's newest whisky distilleries – Glann ar Mor on the rugged (and rather Islay-like) north coast at Pleubian – was funded by trading in them. Jean Donnay, a refugee from the advertising industry in his native Paris, financed his distilling vision by buying stocks of Scottish single malts at 10–12 years old and ageing them for a further two years in Sauternes casks, bottling them under the Celtic Connection brand. And the old stone farmstead he bought on the edge of a rocky bay was, he has said, 'even better than Islay' for maturing whisky. It has the same sea breezes but being 1000-odd miles further south the climate is a good deal milder, with only a few frosts every year.

JUST LIKE THAT

It would surely be every artisan distiller's dream of bliss to have their own neighbourhood cooperage close at hand, bustling with burly crafts persons swiftly and deftly cutting and chamfering and hammering oaken staves as if the last hundred years had simply been erased. Why, English whisky distillers might even revive the old commonplace of having coopers on site... well, no. At the time of writing, and as far as is known, precisely no English distillers have hired full-time coopers – although Bimber of Park Royal, West London, has done the next best thing. Owner Dariusz Plazewski is also an architect and developer, and the workers in his joinery shop have mastered the repair and refurbishment of casks to a high standard. They have even learnt how to toast and rechar, which saves an appreciable amount of time and money. What's important is that Dariusz is both an innovator and a perfectionist and has found uses

Taking a sample, using a whisky thief, at The Oxford Artisan Distillery.

for a house cooper that don't actually involve building new barrels. Repairing and maintaining the ex-bourbon and sherry casks the distillery uses, yes; but as they arrive fully assembled only five weeks after being emptied and at no more than £125-odd each, building new ones would be a criminal waste of money.

No, where the Bimber quasi-coopers have proved their value is in equipping the brewery where the wash is created. Dariusz wanted mashtuns and a washback of American white oak: interaction between cask and new make we already know – it's what makes whisky whisky. But similar interactions can be created further back in the process so that the wash that arrives in the still is already well oaked. His joiners successfully delivered the vessels of upright planking bound with vast iron hoops, which is no mean feat of cooperage even if the tuns need no bilges.

Other distillers either have somebody about the place who can knock a displaced hoop back into place or replace a leaky head or can manage it themselves; more than that, though, and you really need a properly apprenticed and qualified journeyman. The demand is there. The supply of youngsters looking for an alternative living is there. It will happen.

WINE FINISHES

Finishing whisky in old wine barrels, as Jean Donnay did before founding Glann ar Mor, gives the blender an almost inexhaustible repertoire of 'expressions'. Of course, Jean had it easier in at least one sense than his Scottish opposite numbers at the time, in that the Loire and Bordeaux wine regions were a short hop away and actually the Champagne region was not much further. A rich supply of superannuated oak was more or less on his doorstep and he therefore got first pick of whatever was going.

But the availability of flavour-infused old oak only became as important as it is to the mainstream whisky industry in the 1980s and '90s as Scotch's growing popularity around the globe threatened to exhaust its stock of well-matured fillings. Standard blends might have had their malt content tweaked a little in those years – and it's very notable that the smokier of the premium blends, Teacher's and White Horse, stopped being promoted at around that time. As for the premium offerings sought after by the world's wealthy, the spotlight shifted from grand, old, well-aged single distillery malts and alit on new expressions such as Monkey Shoulder and Black Grouse. These had all the cachet and much of the margin of the £20–£30 single malts one might find in a supermarket, and a crisis was averted. Using different types of oak (for instance American Oak or European Oak) played a large part in making these new expressions possible, and it is a way of creating a premium that has stuck.

And it's understandable that playing with barrels, with marriages, and with finishes has caught on at the artisanal end of the spectrum as well as among more mainstream distillers. For a start, the newcomers don't have the luxury of holding back finished whisky until it has achieved venerable status. At three years their new make may not have reached its peak, but it has come of age, it has the key to the door, and it's time it went out and was sold. Most artisan producers will undoubtedly be holding back a fraction of their first releases, if only to see what it does; but for the most part the emphasis is on discovering maturation techniques that make a three-year-old the equal of a five-year-old. These mostly comprise of increasing the contact between wood and spirit either by using smaller barrels or adding oak spindles. One or two even have their new make spending time in chestnut, which is even more porous than oak. Using highly flavoured barrels, particularly ex-port and oloroso, is another way of disguising immaturity, as it used to be for young fogeys when there was such a thing.

Beyond the purely practical side of using oak to give an impression of age, there's a fun side too. In my 40 years in the drinks trade I have seen white wine, vodka, neutral spirit, beer and, most horribly, cider tainted with all sorts of foreign flavourings, mostly fruit-based, to make them palatable to 16-year-old girls. Most recently gins sullied with everything from coconut to pineapple – anything except juniper, that is – have filled the middle shelves. Some see bizarre expressions of whisky as fulfilling a similar function. One who most assuredly doesn't is Abhi Banishek, a lecturer at Heriot-Watt University's International School of Brewing & Distilling for six years before joining and indeed helping to build Chatham's Copper Rivet Distillery in 2016.

For Abhi, it's all about planning and control from the very outset. Copper Rivet has its own strain of barley malted to its requirements, its own chalky boreholes and its own brewhouse complete with master brewer to ensure that wort and wash are rigidly on spec. It's the same with the oak the distillery uses.

'It's a question of keeping control of the flavour at every stage,' says Abhi. 'For instance, slow fermentation and a certain temperature profile will create different sugars. A fruity wort means a fruity wash. In the same way, we are controlling every variable that affects the flavour.'

The same mentality underlies Copper Rivet's rather spartan approach to maturation. 'We only use ex-bourbon casks, with the exception of some virgin white, which accounts for about 2 per cent of our output and is used in one product in particular. We don't rely on the barrel to create the character and we certainly don't try to cover up our mistakes with different finishes!'

In short, Abhi sees whisky as a fully designed and engineered product from wash to cask, and there's absolutely no question of just sticking it in a port barrel and hoping for the best.

THE AGE STATEMENT

It hasn't always been customary, but most malts of any pretension carry an age statement, which is what creates the veneration and awe that attaches to them. The age statement doesn't tell you how old the whisky is. It tells you how old the youngest whisky in the mix was when it went into the bottle. (It must be added that unlike wine, whisky stabilises on bottling and once cork and capsule have been applied, the liquid shouldn't change much until the world ends.)

And with that we must pause for an exposition of one of those regulatory obfuscations so beloved of the Scotch Whisky Association and hardly relevant, therefore, to anything produced south of Berwick.

Once upon a time there were three bears: single malt whisky, being the produce of different years but from a single distillery, mixed with scrupulous care in determined proportions for the sake of consistency; blended whisky, being the alloy of many malt and grain whiskies, again with consistency in mind but also with price, and making up the huge bulk of sales; and finally vatted malt, being a concoction of single malts from various distilleries compounded by a blending house as a deluxe brand. In the days before age statements and what have you, this was as prestigious as a well-aged single malt. These were often referred to by the Sassenach bourgeoisie as 'liqueur whiskies', perhaps inaccurately but a good indicator of their status. The Scotch Whisky Association has now decreed that in order to avoid confusion with blended whiskies, vatted malts must be called blended malts. But only in Scotland.

But we now also have a fourth bear, which has emerged alongside artisan distilling: single cask. Single cask whisky is exactly what it says: it is the product of a single cask which, as it will most likely be a standard US bourbon cask, will hold 200 litres of new-make spirit fresh from the still at 60 per cent abv and above or around 350 70cl bottles at 40 per cent abv. The economics are those of microbrewing: big operators can't make a turn on tiny quantities of niche products, but with the premium an artisan-distilled limited edition can command and the fact the whole run can easily be presold, single cask is deluxe heaven for the smaller fry.

But for most of us, even the cachet of the dates of distillation and bottling prominently displayed on the label can't match the majesty of age.

Snobbery aside, the simple fact is that ageing does something for a whisky. There are no English malts of such magnificent seniority yet, but one day when no-one's looking you can always get your credit card out of the safe and treat yourself to a standard 12-year-old The Glenlivet at £30–40 and a 21-year-old at £15–250. Taste the difference? Well, maybe not £200-worth of difference, but definitely a difference. And there's no magic as to why: up to 70 per cent of the flavour compounds in a well-aged whisky come either directly from the wood or are metabolised by the interaction of wood and spirit. These tend to be the richer, sweeter, fruitier characteristics: mellow, smoky, infused with honey, oak or sherry. Have a care, though! The greater the age, the less discernible the differences become. You need both a keen and an experienced set of papillae to get the full value of that £200 and you may find yourself siding with those who can't really tell three years from 30.

BONDED WAREHOUSES AND MATURATION TIME

If a distillery was an auto engine, the bonded warehouse would be its carburettor. Or possibly its crankshaft. Or at any rate a very important component without which the whole contraption wouldn't work. For if whisky is 70 per cent oak, it's here in the warmth of the barrel's somewhat bitter embrace that the new make has its epiphany. Of course, the watchful Customs officer sees not the mystical metamorphosis but millions of larval pounds, zealously guarded and nurtured while they lie dormant in utero, to become living, breathing tax revenue once safely in vitro. But whether you see these mountain ranges of barrels as magically metaphorical or prosaically fiscal, the bonded warehouse is the distillery's treasure chest.

A bonded warehouse, then, is more than just a building. Much more, in fact: its size, shape, means of construction, location and surroundings all have their effect on the biochemical life in the barrels within, as do the barrels themselves. When we talked of the interaction of spirit and oak, we rather neglected the casks. These come in a range of sizes but only two shapes. The sizes are the quarter at 125 litres, then the barrel (200), the barrique (225), the hogshead (250), the puncheon and the butt (both 500; the former dumpy, the latter tall), the pipe at 550 and the drum at 650 – just short of the 700 litres, which is the maximum barrel size permitted in the UK.

They all have their apologists, but in short the smaller the cask the greater the contact between wood and spirit and the faster the maturation of its contents. The greater contact also quickens the dissipation of spirit vapour through porous oak, which mellows the final product. Smaller casks are also far easier to handle in the warehouse. Supporters of the larger sizes equate the length of maturation with smoothness; and although it would seem that in theory the small cask holds all the aces, in popular sentiment the opposite is true. Few of us mere mortals, it is safe to say, have sensitive enough palates to have a dog in this particular fight.

Inside a dunnage warehouse at The Lakes Distillery.

UPRIGHT OR SIDEWAYS?

The most common types of storage for maturing whisky are either old-fashioned, Scottish-style dunnage warehouses in which the casks are simply stacked on top of each other; or more modern racking in which the casks are stored sideways but on racks, which allows for much higher stacks, and pallet storage, in which as its name suggests the casks are stored on pallets and therefore, crucially, upright. The more modern buildings are climate-controlled and mechanised, whereas old-school dunnage warehouses have to be stoutly built in the interests of stable temperature and humidity, and low-rise for ease of manual handling. The older styles are, of course, much more

picturesque, being generally of rugged stone and slate construction: they tend, therefore, to get turned into the visitor centre, tasting room and gift shop while the piles of barrels themselves are banished to a galvanised steel, agricultural-style prefab hidden behind some trees.

But while one naturally associates these atmospheric old warehouses with their astronomical heritage value with the more handsome of Scotland's malt distilleries, England is – or was – also studded with our equivalent. Victorian England was the largest importer of wine in the world, and all the great seaports had their cellars where the wine was received, assessed for duty and in many cases bottled there. Cellars tended to be chosen for holding wine,

Whisky maturating in the Cotswolds Distillery warehouse.

whatever was warehoused at street level and above, because of their environmental stability; some still serve their original purpose. While its own warehouse was being built, Cotswolds Distillery leased space in just such a cellar in Liverpool, which has also served as an atmospheric set for many films and TV dramas.

Temperature and humidity both impact the speed of evaporation from the casks, which has a knock-on effect on the speed of maturation. The upright/sideways question has a similar impact: the spirit in casks stored vertically evaporates more slowly than it does in a cask stored horizontally for the simple reason that it has a smaller surface area. The dimensions, aspect, degree of insulation and local microclimate all contribute their ha'porth to the environment in which the spirit is going through its evolutions; but as with the shape and size of the barrel, well – I can't tell; can you?

These bottles show the effect of age within the cask over 30 years in relation to colour and what is lost to the Angel's share.

THE ANGEL'S SHARE

Oak's porosity allows some of the ethanol in the barrel to evaporate, helping to blunt the whisky's edge by unmasking other, smoother aromas and flavours. The vapour is famously known as the angel's share; but it's a misnomer because actually the Dominions, Thrones and Powers are always beaten to it by *Baudoinia compniacensis* or whisky fungus. This feeds on the escaping spirit and creates the crusty black fungal colonies that are commonly seen on distillery and more especially warehouse walls. Unsightly these colonies might be, but they are both completely harmless and, given what they feed on, permanently plastered.

CHAPTER SIX

GAZETTEER OF DISTILLERIES

A TOUR AROUND ENGLAND

The visitor centre at Copper Rivet Distillery, based in the Pump House, Chatham Royal Dockyard, Kent.

ENGLISH WHISKY DISTILLERIES

The list below refers first to the number on the facing page map and then the page number for the relevant entry. EWG refers to whether distillery is a member of the English Whisky Guild.

SOUTH-WEST

1. Pocketful of Stones (page 131)
2. Hicks & Healey (page 129)
3. Colwith Farm Distillery (page 127)
4. The Wrecking Coast Distillery (page 135)
5. Princetown Distillers (page 133)
6. Dartmoor Whisky Distillery (page 128)
7. Retribution Distilling Co EWG (page 134)
8. Circumstance Distillery (page 126)

SOUTH AND SOUTH-EAST ENGLAND

9. Witchmark Distillery (page 148)
10. Ten Hides Distillery (page 147)
11. Isle of Wight Distillery (page 144)
12. Canterbury Brewers & Distillers (page 138)
13. Copper Rivet Distillery EWG (page 139)
14. Brightwell Bottle Distillery (page 137)
15. The Oxford Artisan Distillery EWG (page 145)
16. Cotswolds Distillery EWG (page 141)

GREATER LONDON

17. Bimber (page 149) EWG
18. The Old Bakery Gin Distillery (page 153)
19. Doghouse Distillery (page 151)
20. East London Liquor Co EWG (page 151)

EAST OF ENGLAND

21. Adnams Copper House Distillery EWG (page 154)
22. The English Distillery (page 156) EWG

CENTRAL ENGLAND

23. Wharf Distillery (page 165) EWG
24. Spirit of Birmingham (page 163)
25. West Midlands Distillery EWG (page 164)
26. Ludlow Distillery (page 160) EWG
27. Henstone Distillery (page 158) EWG
28. Mercia Distillery & Spirit Lab (page 162)
29. White Peak Distillery (page 167) EWG
30. Elsham Wold Distillery EWG (page 158)

NORTH OF ENGLAND

31. Forest Distillery (page 173)
32. Weetwood Distillery & Brewery (page 177)
33. Whittaker's Distillery (page 179) EWG
34. Cooper King Distillery (page 170) EWG
35. Spirit of Yorkshire Distillery EWG (page 176)
36. Yarm Distillery (page 180) EWG
37. The Lakes Distillery (page 175) EWG
38. Durham Distillery (page 172)
39. Ad Gefrin Distillery (page 169) EWG

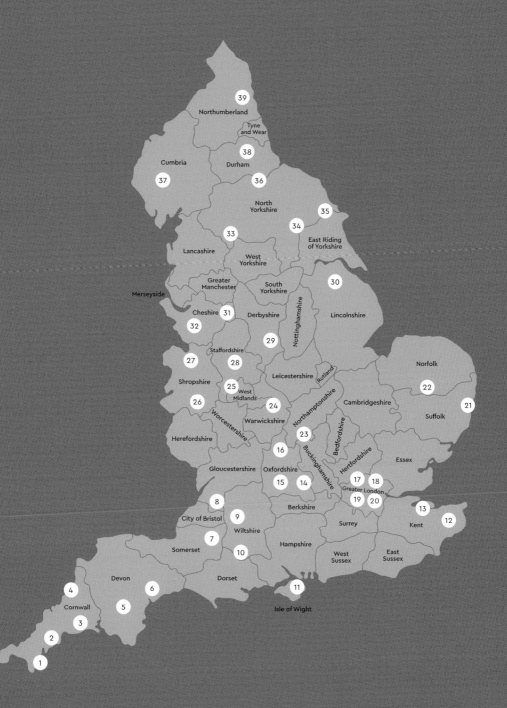

SOUTH-WEST

CIRCUMSTANCE DISTILLERY

📍 *Unit 2, Whitehall Trading Est, Gerrish Ave, Bristol BS5 9DF*

🖥 *Circumstancedistillery.com*

📞 *07743 768091*

💬 *Number 8 on map*

Founded as an offshoot of the city's Psychopomp micro-distillery by brothers Danny and Liam Hirt, Circumstance has been described as 'Britain's most innovative distillery' by the online spirit store Masters of Malt, and on top of that it is about as progressive as it is possible to be. While Psychopomp (the name, according to QI, means 'spirit guide') specialises in gin and vodka and is a partner in a joint venture distilling British akvavit, Circumstance is altogether darker. As well as the usual malted barley Circumstance has produced whiskies from all manner of grains – its first wheat whisky was released in May 2023; there have been rye versions; and it has even dabbled in oats. It also makes rum as well as a premixed Old-Fashioned at 35 per cent abv.

Innovation here goes further than a catholic approach to cereals. As well as the standard ex-bourbon and otherwise seasoned casks Circumstance uses virgin barrels and charred English oak spindles to enhance and control the spirit's maturation. Greater surface contact, as we know, speeds up the maturation and rather nudges at the three-year minimum age, but as they say at Circumstance, when it's ready it's ready. Distillation is on a hybrid pot still with inbuilt four-plate column.

Packaging and distribution do not escape green scrutiny, either: customers can return and refill their lightweight glass bottles, and the hospitality trade is being encouraged to switch from bottles altogether in favour of – horror of horrors! – 5-litre bulk containers. Actually, though, this innovation is not an innovation at all: we have all seen, or at least seen pictures of, Victorian pubs where the spirits are dispensed from decorative (and unbranded) ceramic-fronted barrels or giant bar-top glass dispensers like inverted decanters with a tap at the bottom and a tube down the centre for ice.

Circumstance's commitment to sustainability epitomises the close affinity English whisky distillers have with the environment. Its ingredients, naturally enough, are all organic and are sourced as locally as possible from Warminster Maltings in the next-door county of Wiltshire. Spent grains go to feed the cattle on a neighbouring farm. The distillery itself is certified carbon neutral.

TASTING NOTES

Circumstance Mixed Grain, 50% abv
Nose: Vanilla, white chocolate.
Palate: Savoury hints of oak.
Finish: Bourbon oak and chestnut casks.

Circumstance Single Grain, 42.7% abv
Nose: Floral honey, orchard blossom and cinnamon sugar lead the way, with some savoury rye spice lurking beneath.

Palate: Green apples lead, things stay floral with notes of honeyed baklava, backed by sultanas and buttered pumpernickel.

Finish: Toasted oak and vanilla back up warming ginger and peppercorn spice.

COLWITH FARM DISTILLERY

⚲ *Colwith Farm, Crewell Moor, Pelyn Cross, Lanlivery, Cornwall PL22 0JG*
▯ *Colwithfarmdistillery.co.uk*
☎ *01208 873967*
💬 *Number 3 on map*

Founded in 2015 by the Dustow family to make the Aval Dor range of gins and vodkas from its 400 acres of potatoes (aval dor, literally, means golden apple and is also Cornish for potato), Colwith Farm has evolved into the complete distillery experience. A purpose built still house also shows off its mashtun, three Portuguese hand-beaten copper pot-stills, and two column stills, and includes a visitor centre, tasting room and shop. Experiences include a gin school kitted out with eight mini stills.

A whisky made from the farm's own barley was laid down in 2023 and can be released in 2026 at the earliest.

DARTMOOR WHISKY DISTILLERY

📍 *Old Town Hall, Bovey Tracey, Devon TQ13 9EG*
🖥 *Dartmoorwhiskydistillery.co.uk*
📞 *01626 832874*
💬 *Number 6 on map*

The story of Dartmoor Whisky began in 2009 when Devonian Greg Millar, a conservation plasterer by trade but a whisky-lover by nature, went on a distilling course at Bruichladdich on Islay. Once home he talked to a friend, Simon Crow, about making a whisky from the very high-quality local malting barley and granite-filtered Dartmoor water; and the pair got to work.

The first obstacle they faced – like many other English artisan distillers – was to find a suitable still. Quoted £75,000 for a British-made still they would have to join a two-year queue for, they started looking abroad and in 2014 travelled to the Cognac region where they found the 1966-vintage copper 400-litre pot they still use today. It had been sitting idle since being retired in 1994 but during its working life had made fillings for world-beating top-shelf blends including Rémy Martin, Hennessy and Martel. Now the partners had a pot to... well, to distil in; but they had precious little else.

Fortune, though, favours the brave, and the very next year they struck up a relationship with an industry legend Frank McHardy, a veteran with 50 years in the business under his belt, including long stints at both Springbank, a distillery in Campbeltown and Bushmills in Northern Ireland.

More good luck hit them between the eyes the very next year when Bovey Tracey Town Council quit its HQ since 1866 to move into a modern office in the town's new community hub. Artisan distillers often prefer an eye-catching home with character over a unit on a more convenient industrial estate, and with its stone construction, church-style gothic windows, town-centre site and huge council chamber Greg and Simon would have been lunatics to pass this opportunity up. As well as a working distillery, they hoped it would also prove a powerful attraction, which would help the development of their home town's tourist trade. Restoration work and adaptations were soon completed,

TASTING NOTES

Dartmoor Bourbon Cask, 46% abv
Nose: Fresh pear and peach, with helpings of earthy barley and hay.
Palate: Malty and light, though with a touch of oiliness to it. Vanilla and quince stick around.
Finish: A fleeting hint of smoke, eclipsed by citrus, crunchy brown sugar and desiccated coconut.

with the rather grand council chamber doubling as a spacious stillroom and characterful bar/functions room with the refurbished copper pot as its focal point. In January 2017 the still was ready to start work again after its 23-year dormancy, and before long the very first Dartmoor Whisky was casked. The first bottlings were aged in ex-oloroso casks, one for three years and another for five. Since then, single-cask bottlings aged in ex-bourbon and ex-Bordeaux barrels have been added to the menu, along (of course) with a gin featuring local botanicals such as Dartmoor blueberries.

HICKS & HEALEY

Penhallow, Truro, Cornwall TR4 9LW

healeyscyder.co.uk

01872 573356

Number 2 on map

At some time in your life most of us will experience a phenomenon called vertical integration. A pub that belongs to a brewery. A filling station that belongs to an oil company. That sort of thing. Any enterprise, in short, that both manufactures and retails. Well, this is one. Imagine all the things you might get up to on a Cornish cider (sorry, cyder) farm whose five-bar gates had been thrown open to the emmets. Watching apples being pressed, maybe; guzzling scones and cream and jam (or is that scones and jam and cream?) in the tearoom; snoozing under an apple tree having sampled a few ciders; petting piglets; oh, and nosing some rather good Cornish whisky... doing what? This is supposed to be a cyder farm!

After arriving at Porthallow from a smallholding and off-licence at Mevagissey in 1986, the Healey family – David and Kay, retired since 2017, and sons, Joe and Sam, now in charge – transformed the place, mainly by the sweat of their own brows, from a semi-derelict farm without electricity or mains water into Cornwall's biggest cidermaker, in line with David's original plan. He sold a lot of cider in the shop, mainly from local orchards but with some imported from Devon. It took 10 years of planting, grafting, pruning, picking, milling, pressing and fermenting to get his own output up to 60,000 gallons, and growth has been steady ever since; but he also expanded sideways.

Like Tesco, the Healey philosophy would be to sell everything to everyone everywhere – well, maybe not quite everywhere. But apart from the cider apple trees the Healeys were planting, there were a lot of other fruits to get stuck into. You sell scones? You've got to have jam. Healey's made jam. You made jam? You could make chutney. Healey's made chutney. You had a mill and a press to make your cider? You could make country wines. Healey's made country wines.

The opening of a small distillery was not quite such a natural progression. Since 1990 plenty of English cidermakers have discovered that cider made cider brandy; indeed, English artisan distilling was born in an orchard; but David and Kay hadn't set out to make cider brandy. They wanted to make whisky and in 2003 installed a small copper pot still after talking St Austell Brewery head brewer Roger Ryman into producing the wash to fill it with. Roger, a much admired and much missed man in the industry, had trained in brewing and distilling at Heriot-Watt University and always said he was as interested in the latter as in the former; the wash he made using locally grown Maris Otter barley very nearly made England's first artisanal whisky but was pipped to the post by the English Whisky Company in Norfolk. Roger is no longer with us, alas, but part of his legacy is that St Austell still brews the wash for Hicks & Healey Cornish whisky (the Hicks element being the name of St Austell's founding family). But everything at Porthallow has to earn its living, and today the still makes cider brandy and apple eau de vie as well as a range of three single malt whiskies (one of which is cask strength of 61.3 per cent abv). It makes gin, too, and a few years back it acquired a nearby farm, orchard and vineyard, Tregoninny, whose sparklers have won a fine reputation.

David and Kay's original plan to embrace tourism as warmly as anything can possibly be embraced makes Penhallow an epitome of Cornish tourism. Like many such sites, it tries to do it all: you could almost treat the place as one of those self-contained resorts you don't have to leave. The new visitor centre there boasts a museum with artefacts including a sixteenth-century trough mill and cooper's tools, a tearoom, a shop selling all manner of local produce, a restaurant best described as hearty and a small collection of Austin Healey two-seaters (the clue is in the name). Tours range from a self-guided ramble round the orchard to a veritable odyssey (which should be booked) embracing a look at the press; a peek into the jam factory; a tour of the museum; a look at the still and its cellarage; a tractor ride through the orchards; and a full sampling session. You then retire for the night to Tregoninny, where the farmhouse and a number of cottages have been turned into luxury self-catering.

 TASTING NOTES

Hicks & Healey Single Malt Cornish whiskey, 40% abv
Nose: Spice, honey and barley notes.
Palate: Hints of cocoa, caramel and delicate fruits.
Finish: All rounded off with smooth vanilla.

POCKETFUL OF STONES

📍 *13 Cause Way Head, Penzance TR18 2SN*
🖥 *Pocketfulofstones.co.uk*
📞 *01736 333550*
💬 *Number 1 on map*

You could hardly imagine a more dramatic move than from a Victorian (but very chic) London pub at the foot of the Telecom Tower in up-and-coming Fitzrovia in central London to darkest Cornwall. But that's what Shaun Bebington of the Lukin in Conway Street and his Hungarian chef Balasz Schieber did when they founded Pocketful of Stones.

Shaun, a South African with a love of surfing, was also an inveterate dabbler who had been toying with botanicals on a little test-still in the Lukin's cellar. He once made whisky out of some short-date Doom Bar and pronounced it delicious. In 2016, after a family bereavement and under intolerable pressure at work, he felt a yearning for cleaner air and more open skies than Fitzrovia could offer. He had grown up two minutes from the beach in Durban, surfing and building sandcastles; and after the death of his mother he decided he needed a change of pace and a lungful of sea air. Combining his urge to escape with his penchant for whisky he left Fitzrovia to its own devices while he and Balasz upcycled their skills to run a bar and distillery pretty much on the edge of the Atlantic where surf is, very often, up.

Pocketful of Stones's handmade Portuguese copper pots, one 700 litres and one 500 litres, may not produce much in the way of quantity, but they work their little cotton socks off to produce variety. There's a cider brandy; an absinthe at 66 per cent abv made with locally grown wormwood and named after a local mermaid, Morveren; a summer cup whose charge of soft fruits changes throughout the growing season; dandelion and burdock, damson, marmalade, hop and squid ink – yes, squid ink – gins; and the original dry gin, Caspyn, which is not actually named after a nearby stone circle at all. The stone circle is really called the Nine Merry Maidens, but Sean and Balasz were misled by the fact that it is managed by the Cornish Ancient Sites Protection Network, whose initials are prominently displayed at the entrance to the site.

The distillery's whisky is named Hell's Stone after the charter myth of neighbouring Helston, home of the floral or furry dance, a tale that involves the Devil, the Archangel Michael, a huge flaming boulder and a battle in the sky. The wash is actually an unhopped porter made by the St Ives microbrewery and is highly rated as a beer in its own right; Shaun has worked with several Cornish microbreweries and has also had a go at a collaboration, producing a blended whisky with Loch Lomond distillery in the Scottish Highlands.

'The freedom to improvise is very important and very exciting, but at heart I'm a traditionalist,' he says. 'Whisky is what it is because of the experience and work of many generations, so we pay heed to the people who have come before us. We're not trying to rub people up the wrong way.'

Pocketful of Stones is not really visitable on its edge-of-town industrial estate. However, the eponymous town-centre pub is eminently visitable and is the venue for regular tastings.

Oh, and one last thing... the name. Traditionally, upset and depressed people weigh down their pockets with stones before walking into the sea, a tip that Reggie Perrin clearly hadn't heard of while Pip in *Great Expectations* clearly had. Luckily for the world, Shaun may have been at a low ebb when he chose the name, but self-evidently never quite that low; and with the reviving power of clean air all around him, a clear sky above unobstructed by the BT Tower, and a suitably rumpled sea at his feet, he's as happy now as you will be after trying his whisky.

 TASTING NOTES

Hell's Stone Whisky, 40% abv

Nose: Sweet vanilla and toasted nuts with wafts of soft, aged oak.

Palate: Honey granola and almond croissants, a hint of zesty orange with underlying seaweed.

Finish: Vanilla custard, creamy malt and roasted nuts, with warming spice on the finish.

PRINCETOWN DISTILLERS

📍 *Station Rd, Princetown, Yelverton PL20 6QY*
🖥 *www.dartmoor.com*
📞 *0203 371 8656*
💬 *Number 5 on map*

If all goes according to plan, then in a very few years' time Dartmoor is going to be English whisky's Highland Region and Princetown will be its Tomintoul. At a reputed initial cost of £8 million (and doubtless far more to come), Princetown represents one of the biggest investments in English whisky to date and has been funded mainly from private venture capital, along with a busy trade in cask futures. Its four washbacks can churn out 30,000 litres at a time each; its wash still has a capacity of 19,500 litres; its spirit still is scarcely much smaller at 13,500 litres; and its warehouse can squeeze in 1000 slumbering casks.

Princetown may be among the front rank of English whisky distilleries in terms of size, but one superlative it can claim as all its own is altitude. At 420 metres it boasts a low air-pressure that will allow low-temperature distillation, which not only saves energy but also allows fine cuts for a smoother end product. The water is also pretty clean hereabouts, far higher up the hill than the point where the water board can fill it with raw sewage.

It has to be admitted that Princetown has had a troubled birth. Conceived by mining engineer Rowan Maule, it was incorporated as long ago as 2015 and was scheduled to open – at a cost of a mere £4 million – in 2019. Of course, it didn't happen; but it wasn't so much the planning process, complicated by being in a national park, that scuppered the original plan. There were objections to its Doig-style dummy pagoda as not being appropriate to Dartmoor – unlike the barracks of a prison in the same village! – and of course someone was trotted out to say that Dartmoor wasn't the right place for a distillery even though it's the perfect place for a distillery.

But all were swept aside by the imminent closure of the prison and the loss of all its jobs. Princetown won't provide as many jobs, but it will create rather more visitors than the prison did, and ones who are free to spend in shops and pubs at that! But add Covid to the usual list of hitches and hiccups and – well, its first spirit was laid down in 2022 and will be with us when altitude and humidity allow. And two people who'll be particularly pleased when the cash tills start to ring are the Prince and Princess of Wales: in their capacities as Duke and Duchess of Cornwall they are also its landlords.

RETRIBUTION DISTILLING CO

📍 *85 Oakfield Rd, Frome, Somerset BA11 4JH*
🖥 *Retributiondistilling.co.uk*
📞 *07974 015846*
💬 *Number 7 on map*

We have already noted that while craft brewers and artisan gin distillers have the luxury – within limits – of being able to play with all sorts of variations in method and ingredient, the three-year rule and the strict prescriptions enshrined in law between them leave whisky distillers with rather less latitude. Still, you can't stop some people, and if their concoction of oatmeal stout-based wash, vacuum-distilled and aged in ex-arak casks fails (as it surely will) – well, it was only a single cask, and the spirit can always be repurposed as hand sanitiser.

One such unstoppable spirit is Richard Lock, founder of Retribution Brewery, which almost immediately became Retribution Distillery Co. A hydrographer in the oil and gas industry, Richard was also a prominent marathon runner whose career was ended by injury and who entered the booze business (while keeping his day job) as a sideline. Think that makes him an amateur? Think again! He started homebrewing in 2011 and took his hobby as far as the International Centre for Brewing & Distilling at Edinburgh's Heriot-Watt University before the sporting injury prompted his big change of direction. That the change of direction pretty much coincided with the arrival of Covid-19 didn't even slow him down.

In that short time he has designed and built his own column still; experimented with all sorts of grains and malts, yeasts and combinations of yeasts, fermentation practices, methods of distillation and barrel types; and turned out dry gin, Navy gin, hazy lemon gin, gin-based summer cup, white rum and spiced rum. He laid down his first whisky at Christmas 2020 and at the time of writing had committed to oak five further single-cask malts, made on his hand-built direct-fired copper pots and without chill-filtering or colour equalisation. And all this while still working as a hydrographer. There can be few distillers as energetic as Richard, and few minds as restless and fertile. But then, nascent industries are built on such human dynamos.

THE WRECKING COAST DISTILLERY

📍 *Unit 2 Pentire Workshops, Highfield Rd Ind Est, Delabole, Cornwall PL33 9BA*
🖥 *Thewreckingcoastdistillery.com*
📞 *No telephone number listed; email: info@thewreckingcoastdistillery.com*
💬 *Number 4 on map*

They could have called it the Rabbithole Distillery and they wouldn't have been far out, because just as one Google search leads inevitably to another and you end up losing half the day, so one botanical grist led to another until the founders of The Wrecking Coast ended up with a clotted cream gin in their portfolio.

Craig Penn and Avian Sandercock were fellow rugby club members in London, sharing not just a love of the oval ball but also a passion for gin, and not just sampling different gins critically but also dabbling in making various botanical grists of their own. This continued even when Avian and his family moved to Cornwall, because the Penns quickly discovered the delights of the county's Atlantic coast and used to visit them there when they could. Gin-tasting sessions were part of the curriculum of these visitations, and after one such visit the guys started talking about the possibility of setting up on their own. Go on then, we dare you, said their wives.

So they did.

The Wrecking Coast's first home was a disused garage in the basement of a bakery in Tintagel where Avian operated the bells and whistles and Craig, a marketing man by trade, kept the whole thing afloat. The partners had been great beer-lovers but had migrated to spirits, and while Craig remained a whisky-lover they decided at first to major in gin. They had great fun experimenting with all sorts of locally grown fruit and veg, as craft gin distillers are wont to do; and, of course, foraged herbs such as the vitamin C-laden scurvy grass and other weeds that came to hand. This all culminated in the celebrated clotted cream gin, the drink for which The Wrecking Coast is still best-known, the clotted cream being introduced to the gin by use of a vacuum still and other such ungodly and unnatural contrivances.

The garage was soon outgrown, and the kit was first transferred, swelling as it went, to a unit in Delabole and finally to a former chemical factory in Camelford where it remains, and where there is a lab so that Avian need never see the light of day again. Here the duo started making various rums, including one infused with the damson-like Kea plum, once an important local cash crop but today only found in a single orchard in the village of Kea.

All this time they had been plotting whiskey, but with an 'e' because they were after something new world rather than a Scotch clone. To this end they brought over some German rye whiskey to try different finishes. The results are two 8-year-olds, one finished in sherry casks, one in bourbon, as well as an overproof Cornish single malt distilled from wash made by a local microbrewer.

The Wrecking Coast remains primarily a gin distillery with whiskey in its portfolio rather than, as is so often the case, a whisky distillery with a gin in its portfolio. But the innovative spirit that gave us clotted cream gin still shines through.

Footnote: It is a myth that villagers on Cornwall's wild Atlantic coast would set fake beacons on stormy nights to lure hapless cargo ships onto the rocks, whereupon they would strip the stricken vessels of anything and everything they could carry home, murder the mariners and act all innocent next day. Beacons and other lights are there for the opposite purpose – to warn off rather than attract. What is true is that when there was a wreck the villagers would indeed strip it bare, as the then operative laws of salvage allowed; they tended to rescue rather than murder the sailors, though.

 TASTING NOTES

The Wrecking Coast Rye Whiskey, 50.5% abv

Nose: Toasted spices and silky honey waft among buttered toast, burnt caramel and cooking herbs, followed by tangy berries and gentle black pepper.

Palate: Sweet summer fruits and darker juicy currants, with herbaceous zest in tow. Earthy spice and cacao build, with liquorice, drying oak and tangy dried raspberries.

Finish: Dark, charred sugar, fragrant anise, more forest fruits and just a hint of fresh mint.

SOUTH & SOUTH-EAST

BRIGHTWELL BOTTLE DISTILLERY

📍 *Highlands Farm, Brightwell, Wallingford OX10 0QX*

🖥 *www.bbdistillery.co.uk*

📞 *07985 267972*

💬 *Number 14 on map*

Founded by engineering contractor Tony Reilly on his farm in 2015, Brightwell has something of a low profile partly because Tony is still contracting, partly because Brightwell Vineyard in the same village also distils – in its case Rush brandy – and partly because it's better known by its original name, Black Bottle Distillery. Under this name it distilled the well-known IQ gin, which had to be changed because there's already a very old-established blended Scotch of the same name. As well as the twin Randolph whiskies (below), there is another single malt, Oscar Wilde at 45 per cent abv.

 TASTING NOTES

Lord Randolph Oxford Malt, 45% abv
Nose: A hint of dry spice, with lemon blossom, fresh malt, digestive biscuits and a touch of caramel.
Palate: Citrus returns, with orange milk chocolate, dry oak and heather honey.
Finish: Floral malt and lemon shortbread.

Randolph Oxford Barrel Proof, 58% abv
Nose: Chocolate orange, black pepper, pine and toffee.
Palate: Powerfully malty, with more citrus and toasted spices.
Finish: Lingering hints of cinnamon and chocolate peanuts.

CANTERBURY BREWERS & DISTILLERS

📍 *The Foundry Brewpub, 77 Stour St, Canterbury Kent CT1 2NR*
🖥 *Thefoundrycanterbury.co.uk*
📞 *01227 455899*
💬 *Number 12 on map*

That precious rarity, a boutique bar-distillery that makes whisky as well as gin, the Foundry has the additional advantage of occupying one of the best possible locations in the country. The pub takes up part of a historic cast-iron foundry almost on the river front and bang-slap in the city centre. Drury & Bigglestone's closed in the 1960s after 150-odd years in operation, during which time it produced the world's first electric lamp standards and built the water towers for the Deal to Chatham railway. It was converted in 2011 by Jon and Jodie Mills into an all-singing, all-dancing brewpub with cider press and restaurant celebrating Kentish heritage and produce right in the shadow of Canterbury Cathedral itself.

The addition of a distillery has given Jon, who operates it, a chance to show off a truly inventive flair and to produce one beverage that is so new it doesn't even have a name. The Foundry has a range of gins with the sort of esoteric botanical characters we have almost come to expect from craft distillers; it has a vodka; it has both white and spiced rums. So far so good. And then it has Moonshine, a grain spirit let down to 44.5 per cent abv with its own cider and local fresh-pressed apple juice and then sat on a nest of cinnamon for a few weeks to get spicy. Now what do you call that? It's not gin, it's not vodka, it's not a liqueur... in fact there's only one thing you can call it: 'Same again, please'.

In 2018 or thereabouts Jon bought himself a new toy, a 100-litre still in which to have a go at a small-batch (very small batch) whiskey (the 'e' reflecting his new-world influences). It was released in March 2023 under the brand name Streetlight, commemorating the Foundry's prehistory. 'It was a labour of love, really,' says Jon; but it was a labour of inquisitiveness, too, for its yeast did not come from the home-brew shelf at Wilko. A team of biochemists from Canterbury Christ Church University had been working at St Augustine's Abbey, the site where the saint and his mission first settled on their arrival in Kent in 597. The scientists found 100 spores of yeast and similar micro-organisms – just imagine the lambic you'd get from that! – of which four were still viable and found their way to the Foundry. This is the very same yeast St Augustine and his chums fermented their ale with more than 1400 years ago! This is not the first such trial of laboratory-cultured old yeasts: residue from ancient Egyptian pots has been similarly resurrected. But St Augustine! Wow is all.

Jon's strategy with his whiskies will mirror his strategy with beer: keep ringing the changes. He aims to release several single-cask variations a year, each as different and surprising as possible. Already snoozing in their used bourbon casks are rye, corn and mixed-grain whiskies; and a new make mashed from an 8.5 per cent abv imperial stout is said to be coming along nicely. And contrary to received wisdom Jon will be experimenting with coloured brewing malts. Jon understands the argument that so much of the flavour of whisky comes from the wood that messing about with coloured malts makes no difference to the end product; but he maintains that having the courage of your convictions and using crystal by the shovelful – yes, it makes a difference.

COPPER RIVET DISTILLERY

📍 *Pump House no. 5, Chatham Dockyard, Leviathan Way, Chatham ME4 4LP*
🖥 *Copperrivetdistillery.com*
📞 *01634 931122*
💬 *Number 13 on map*

The Copper Rivet story began way back in 1979 when the Russell family Bob, Matt and Stephen opened a wine bar in Rainham, Kent. The bar grew to become the headquarters of a wines and spirits importer and distributor, and the family conceived a notion that the next step might be a distillery of their very own.

The idea was a long time maturing but accelerated after 2012 when Stephen was introduced to Abhi Banichek. Abhi, a teacher at the International Centre for Brewing & Distilling at Edinburgh's Heriot-Watt University and an active consultant to artisan distillery start-ups, had some pretty radical ideas of his own, including a column still 10 metres tall, called Joyce, and another somewhat shorter version, Janet, which Abhi designed himself. Together with the pot, Sandy, which doubles as both wash and spirit still, they took up a fair few square metres and the hunt for a roof to put over their heads took the team all over England and into Scotland. Eventually they came across the ideal home in their own back yard: on a day out with his family Matthew discovered that an impressive former pumphouse in the Chatham Historic Dockyard was vacant and for sale, and it was no contest.

Built in 1873, it had originally housed the mighty hydraulic pumps that drained three of Chatham's dry docks and drove all the cranes, capstans and other machinery. Even with the stills and ancillary gear all plumbed in there was still space for a brewhouse wherewith to make the wash; so as you can imagine and will one day, perhaps, see for yourself, the scale is pretty heroic.

The ribbon having been cut by the Princess Royal, the stills were charged in late 2016 and torrents of limpid gin and crystal-clear vodka promptly started flowing. At the same time a number of whiskies were laid down, starting with a fairly conventional single malt dubbed Masthouse – no, not Malthouse! –

after one of the shipbuilding activities the dockyard had once hosted. Other manifestations, however, are not so conventional. Masthouse was released in 2020 and has been followed by a grain whisky with a sweet, nutty and spicy grist of unmalted barley, wheat and rye with just enough malted barley to power the starch conversion. This, too, has become more conventional since the days when grain whisky was Scotch's dirty secret; but then we slip the surly bonds of earth and explode into space with an unprecedented column-distilled single malt. This is the kind of 'why not?' thinking that will help put English whisky's mark on the world!

The pumphouse is not only big enough for all the brewing and distilling paraphernalia, it's also big enough for a restaurant. Copper Rivet markets its visitor offering as very much part of the Historic Dockyards experience, so you can have a day out comprising a distillery tour (must be booked), a good lunch, a bottle of something out of the ordinary to take home, and a few moments' solemn contemplation at the birthplace of HMS Victory as well.

 TASTING NOTES

Masthouse Single Malt, 45% abv

Nose: Apple and peachy fruit with cereal notes like malt and oats, with vanilla, cinnamon, marzipan and a lift of lemon peel.

Palate: Creamy, with a full cereal texture, some peppery alcohol, you can feel the abv. Smooth and round with porridge, chocolate digestive biscuits and that citrus peel note again.

Finish: Vanilla comes through strongly with oatcakes and custard. It's smooth as hell and packed with flavour.

Masthouse Grain Whisky, 42% abv

Nose: Toasted nuts, cinnamon porridge and light biscuity sweetness.

Palate: Vanilla shortbread, nutty brown bread, mint creams and earthy spices.

Finish: Soft, creamy vanilla and herbal rye spices.

COTSWOLDS DISTILLERY

Phillips Field, Whichford Rd, Shipston-on-Stour, Warwickshire CV36 5EX

cotswoldsdistillery.com

01608 238 533

Number 16 on map

Cotswolds Distillery doesn't feel like a distillery and isn't even all that 'Cotswoldy'. The buildings, for a start, have an almost Scandinavian newness about them. They're constructed of the appropriate Cotswold stone, of course, but they're clean-cut, unfussy and as untwee as they can be. Nothing that a bit of moss and some hanging baskets won't cure in due course, though: people expect Cotswold stone to mellow and become charmingly bosky, and mellow and charmingly bosky is what they will eventually get.

And although the northern Cotswolds are pretty enough they're much more workaday than the showpiece towns and villages further south, where even the sprogs' pedalcars are four-wheel drive and the cleaners have to be bussed in from Swindon. Even so, there's something a bit strange about the fact that there's a distillery here at all, and not unnaturally its very existence caught the attention of visitors to one of England's most visited regions. Soon after opening in 2014 founder Dan Szor, a former City financier, started running guided tours and tastings. In 2015 he and his team received 7000 visitors, and before long the number rose to 30,000. But there was scarcely any space for the tastings, let alone a post-tour cuppa, so the distillery now has a purpose-built visitor centre with comfortable tasting rooms more like the foyer of a well-appointed hotel, a terrace, a shop stocked with all manner of local produce, and a café that offers simple but top-notch snacks and light meals. Visitor numbers are off the scale and tours, as you can imagine, must be booked.

New Yorker Dan spent 26 years as a currency trader, mostly in Paris and London, before his eureka moment hit him on a trip to Bruichladdich on Islay in May 2013. Ten years earlier he'd bought a cask to lay down and was on his annual pilgrimage to pat it and stroke it when he mentioned to manager Jim McEwan that he'd been thinking about founding a distillery of his own. Jim simply told him to get on with it and recommended him to Master Distiller Harry Cockburn, veteran of 15 start-ups across the globe; and suddenly the project was flying.

'I spoke to Jim on the Friday, rang Harry on the Sunday, and on the Monday we were in Sweden looking at second-hand equipment,' says Dan.

The speed at which events moved from then on were probably less terrifying to a City trader than they would be to the rest of us; but a mere 14 months later Dan was able to fire up his 500-litre Holstein gin rectifying still while his two Forsyth copper pot stills – a 2400-litre wash still and a 1600-litre spirit still

– were only waiting to be connected to the gas before his first batch of new-make whisky dripped out of the condenser.

Luck, it must be said, played its part in the breakneck pace of developments; although it must also be said that fortune favours the brave, and much of Dan's 'luck' was a product of his energy, his business experience and acumen, and his access to some pretty substantial chunks of capital. Exactly the right premises in the form of a newly built house and barn that were empty thanks to a planning wrangle, came on the market just five miles away from Dan and his neurologist wife Katia's country home. That was luck. That Dan was in a position to pounce on it wasn't. The house (built on a planning grant of light industrial use, hence the wrangle) was absolutely perfect for the laboratory, offices and shop; the barn is among the most spacious new-wave still houses in the land; and a brand-new and rather luxurious visitor centre with café, shop and tasting rooms is, after the big hiccup that was Covid, back in action as the starting and finishing point for tours and the venue for tastings and masterclasses.

The two Forsyth stills also materialised by a stroke of luck. Having given up on the second-hand Swedish equipment they were scouting Dan and Harry resigned themselves to an indeterminate spell on Forsyth's waiting list when suddenly the phone rang – a cancellation; would they like to...? Yes they would. And yes, they could.

Almost the last piece of the puzzle fell into place when Dan and Harry decided to source their malt from Warminster, whose boss introduced them to a local farmer with 2000 acres of organic Odyssey barley to dispose of. Warminster, one of the few traditional floor maltings left in Britain, is able to guarantee provenance by batch-malting, which means that Cotswold can genuinely proclaim its whisky to be as local to its terroir as any Scottish single malt. Then Dan heard that the Malvern Mineral Water spring had been closed three years earlier, and promptly had it reopened. So the barley and the water are truly local, but only because Dan had made sure he had the resources to exploit unexpected opportunities.

The casks are foreigners – bourbon barrels from Speyside Cooperage for the first fill, then Dan had hoped to mature his stocks in the Cotswolds, too, but at first he couldn't find a suitable bond. He approached the Bristol Spirit Company, which couldn't oblige but directed him to Liverpool, where Plutus – an atmospheric Victorian bonded warehouse on the city's docks, which has served as a film location more than once – rented him a corner of its brick-vaulted cellars where his casks snuggled up against 10,000 barrels of rum until 2017. By this time his Founders' Circle had raised much of the £2,500,000 Dan needed to pay for the building of an on-site bonded warehouse and the purchase of two shops, one opposite the world-renowned Lygon Arms Hotel in Broadway and the second in the Cotswolds' Capital of Cute, Bourton-on-the-Water.

What has this 'grass to glass' combination of Cotswold malt, Malvern water and clean fresh country air created? 'I love maritime peaty malts, but here we have got a definite terroir,' says Dan. 'This is a beautiful, rolling, fertile area so the notes ought to be grain and fruit with vanilla, honey, raisins, Christmas cake – a lighter whisky, blonde rather than brunette, but with plenty of depth.' Are his wide-necked stills with their steeply angled lyne arms giving him that? Well, that's for you to judge: a range of different expressions of his single malt is ready, although the new make is still being bottled too. But the Holstein still is earning its living with Cotswold Dry Gin. And a range of specials flavoured from a library of 100 botanicals, some of them, such as the red hemp nettle (actually a mint) indigenous to the area. It is, says Dan, all about taste.

TASTING NOTES

Cotswolds Single Malt, 46% abv

Nose: The first thing you notice are spicy cereal notes, malt and porridge, then comes the fruit – orange peel and lemon. Grassy and floral flavours followed by marzipan.

Palate: Beautiful texture, creamy and round, with sweet citrus fruit and black pepper.

Finish: Good length. There's vanilla custard and a lift of aromatic freshness that will make you want another sip.

Cotswolds Founder's Choice Single Malt, 59.1% abv

Nose: Soft peach and juicy pear, tropical notes of grilled mango, herbal honey and chocolate coffee beans.

Palate: A warming kick of ginger builds, accompanied by dustings of cinnamon and dark chocolate. Roasty coffee balances sweet, nutty notes with delicate hints of zesty marmalade.

Finish: Fruity banana bread, still tropical and additional layers of summer fruit berries are followed by a good helping of creamy barley.

Cotswolds Bourbon Cask Single Malt, 59.1% abv

Nose: Vanilla custard, green apple and a hint of toasted oak smokiness.

Palate: Peanut brittle, sultana, shortbread and cinnamon.

Finish: Buttery biscuits, white pepper and orange zest.

ISLE OF WIGHT DISTILLERY

Pondwell Hill, Ryde PO33 1PX

isleofwightdistillery.com

01983 613653

Number 11 on map

The wine-lover's loss became the whisky-lover's gain in the Isle of Wight when Conrad Gauntlett, founder nearly 40 years ago of the 30-acre Rosemary Vineyard near Ryde, threw in his lot with Xavier Baker of local Goddard's Brewery in 2014 to found the Isle of Wight Distillery, the first ever, as far as records show, on the island.

It was a well-timed move: Isle of Wight was one of seven new English distilleries to open that year, and the gin boom was really hitting its stride. The distillery's Mermaid Gin was a big hit just as the flags were being lowered for the vineyard: a planning application for 150-ish homes on the site was submitted in 2017 and the Rosemary Vineyard site has now been redeveloped.

Meanwhile, the stills had been set up in an old pub, the Wishing Well, just uphill from the village aptly known as Seaview. The stills are separated from the stone-flagged Mermaid Bar only by a glass screen, so tours are not really a goer; but there are regular short talks followed by free tastings. (Tables must be booked.) The products include a navy-strength dark rum, a dry gin, a pink gin, a navy-strength gin and a barrel-aged gin. The locally sourced botanicals include Boadicea hops and samphire.

A single malt whisky made with Island-grown barley was laid down in 2015 even before the gin was launched. The wash was brewed at Goddard's and cool-fermented at 24°C compared to the more usual 40°C for a smoother palate. It has been maturing in bourbon barrels and is due to be finished in white wine casks and cut with Island spring water, but at the time of writing no decision had been made on when.

THE OXFORD ARTISAN DISTILLERY

📍 *Old Depot, South Park, Cheney Lane, Headington, Oxford OX3 7QJ*
🖥 *theoxfordartisandistillery.com*
📞 *01865 767918*
💬 *Number 15 on map*

Given how stuffed it is with the old grey matter, the city of Oxford really ought to be equally stuffed with imagination, innovation, ingenuity, intuition and all that other intellectual stuff. And, at least as far as whisky (or in this case, whiskey) is concerned, it is.

Known affectionately as TOAD, the distillery was found in 2017 by music industry entrepreneur Tom Nicolson and a veritable Brains Trust of the artisan movement including distillers Cary Mason and Tagore Ramoutar (now a non-executive director at the Wiltshire Distilling Company and a leading light in the English Whisky Guild), heritage grower George Bennett of Thame, who'll whip you up a wash of Bronze Age emmer in two shakes of an aurochs's tail, and archaeobiologist John Letts who, believe it or not, discovered many heritage cereal strains concealed in medieval thatched roofs and was able to revive them as viable crops.

The list of trades – there aren't that many archaeobiologists in the distilling business – is a bit of a giveaway: together they add up to curiosity, knowledge and disrespect for convention. Take TOAD's stills, for instance. Inspired by the cut-down steam boilers improvised from scrapped loco engines by Haitian distillers, the crew at TOAD, along with the engineers from South Devon Railway (formerly Dart Valley), designed and built Nautilus, a 2400-litre monster, and Nemo, a more modest 500 litres. The array is completed by two five-metre 40-plate columns. These are the same engineers who refurbished the Flying Scotsman, so they know what they're about.

Home for what might be described as this installation is a Grade II listed barn in Oxford's South Park (don't worry – no Kenny was killed in the making of this distillery), which doubles as a social hub for the park's users and neighbours. There is a café, which welcomes passing dogwalkers, joggers and tai chi practitioners as well as distillery visitors on tours and tastings. There is an al fresco bar, open when clement. It's got public loos, too, all at TOAD's expense. It's even got a bakery – an artisan one, of course, so if you don't like sourdough keep walking.

The bulk of the output thus far has been small-batch rye gin and vodka. TOAD has also contract-distilled for the likes of the Oxford Botanical Gardens; the Highgrove Estate and a string of local hotels and restaurants are happy to pay a bit extra for the exclusive labels that their patrons are just as happy to pay a lot extra for.

But what we are here for is, of course, the whiskey (note the spelling, which generally denotes a spirit of independence from Scotland.) Numbered single-cask editions of rye whiskey were first released in 2021. Now, TOAD is brandishing heritage grain whiskies like a Highlander with a claymore. As well as the (comparatively) straightforward Oxford Rye there's Purple Grain, Easy Ryder, Red Red Rye, Crafty Little Rye and doubtless many more expressions by the time you read this; then there's a Heritage Corn Spirit and, this being Oxford, The Graduate. Many of these are export or even cask proof: Oxford Tawny Pipe is a cask-proof rye finished in a tawny port pipe and bottled at 56 per cent abv.

Oh, and as well as being expert distillers, the TOAD crew are expert brewers: all their wash is mashed and fermented on site.

TASTING NOTES

Oxford Rye Whisky #2, 53.6% abv

Nose: Toffee pennies, almond and walnut, red liquorice, cooked orchard fruit and familiar peppery heat.

Palate: Richly fruity with redcurrant and blackberry, though the earthiness of the rye still manages to sneak through. Honey and vanilla remains.

Finish: Spicy cardamom and cassia, with a touch of fried banana.

Oxford Rye The Tawny Pipe, 56% abv

Nose: Plenty of red fruits, juicy blackberries, dried figs, with sticky malt loaf and nutty grist.

Palate: Silky caramel, with spiced apple compote, chewy dates and prunes.

Finish: Peppery rye spice builds, with delicate meadow herbs.

TEN HIDES DISTILLERY

📍 *14 Avonside, New Broughton Road, Melksham SN12 8BT*

🖥 *Tenhides.com*

📞 *07817 868252*

💬 *Number 10 on map*

There's no better way of discovering an unfamiliar landscape than being forced to eat it. No, really. Just ask former soldier Andrew Wilson who, despite being born and raised a Yorkshireman with all the complications that entails, fell in love with Wiltshire after being repeatedly obliged to fall to its loamy bosom and press his face deep into it. Such intimate contact with the topography and flora of a landscape undeveloped thanks to its hidden lodes of high explosive is bound to engender a certain fondness. At any rate, after service in Germany, Northern Ireland, Iraq and Afghanistan, all soothed by the army officer's traditional fortifying dram, Andrew found himself longing for Salisbury Plain.

After his discharge Andrew found work distilling gin in Aberdeen but eventually made his way back to Wiltshire with some useful experience under his belt and whisky on his mind. Tinhead Distillery was founded in the middle of the Covid pandemic in farm buildings near Devizes, but with plague ravaging the land it wasn't a good time, everything was dragged out, and Andrew got by at first on contract-distilled gin and spiced rum. His own still – a 300-litre handmade Slovenian pot of the right quality and price, because for some reason British fabricators don't seem able to keep up with demand – arrived only in March 2022, by which time the fledgling firm had found a new home in a 1950s dairy on the river in Melksham with bar and a terrace on which to enjoy the selection of whiskies. The distillery had meanwhile been rechristened Ten Hides, the original Anglo-Saxon name for the part of Devizes where it was first set up. (A hide means either enough ploughland to feed a household or its notional yield on which rent and tax were calculated, so the original Ten Hides was probably a middling thegn's estate.)

Andrew's Slovenian pot was commissioned in late 2023 with the active assistance of experienced consultant Jack Mayo, and charged with a wash from the Three Daggers brewery in nearby Edington, then filled into old wine barrels to mature which, Andrew hopes, will lead in good time to a 'very smooth, rounded whisky with a rich, full palate'. It's going to be a long wait before we find out. But being as it's made from Icknield series barley, which is the best barley in the world, and cut with Wiltshire Downs chalk-filtered spring water, which is the purest water in the world, it'll be worth it.

WITCHMARK DISTILLERY

📍 *Fonthill Estate, Tisbury SP3 5SF*

🖥 *witchmark.co.uk*

📞 *01747 356110*

💬 *Number 9 on map*

One thing every gentleman needs is a brewery-cum-distillery at the gate of his stately home, so that whenever he fancies a snifter he can send a footman down the drive to fetch him one. Poor chap might not be back for some time, but that's just one of the burdens of greatness.

Anyway, the 3rd Baron Margadale has been able to boast exactly that luxury since 2020, when the well-established and well-regarded Keystone Brewery in the old carpentry shop on his 9000-acre Fonthill estate joined forces with businessmen Alistair Munro and John Caron to found The Wiltshire Distilling Company. A single malt, a single grain and a rare blend are asleep in the oak for now, so here's nothing to taste at time of writing, but the omens look good. The local barley grows on soil of the esteemed Icknield series type; the water is filtered through chalk; the bespoke copper stills were hand-made in Italy; the visitor centre and shop are housed in a picturesque grain-drying shed (although shed is perhaps not the right word) adjoining the grade II-listed barn in which the distillery itself is housed.

And the hands-on guy is one to trust, too: Eddie Large and his wife Charlie founded Keystone here in 1986 and have built up a strong following in the area's pubs, which they hope to retain; but you won't hear the name Keystone any more. And thereby hangs a tale. The stone walls of the host buildings are covered in witches' marks, the apotropaic good luck symbols scratched by workers in the super-superstitious sixteenth and seventeenth centuries to ward off – well, witches mainly, but all manner of mishap and mischief besides. Health and safety Tudor and Stuart-style, to be flippant. The ones you see here are of the daisywheel pattern, which is why Keystone Brewery is now Stone Daisy Brewery.

The whiskies when they emerge (if they haven't already) will sell under the Witchmark brand, which is a trifle misleading since the word witchmark commonly meant a mole or birthmark on the suspect's skin that the witchfinder would prick with an awl to confirm her guilt. But whether strictly accurate or not, it all draws on the district's rich folklore and enhances the savour of the drink exactly as a good ghost story enhances the ambience of a stately home. The distillery will be operational by spring 2024.

GREATER LONDON

BIMBER

📍 *56 Sunbeam Rd NW10 6JQ*
🖥 *bimberdistillery.co.uk*
📞 *020 3602 9980*
💬 *Number 17 on map*

If you had to sit down with a blank sheet of A4 – okay, a blank screen – and put yourself together a wish list of what you'd like to find at the archetypal English whisky distillery, you'd come up with something very like Bimber.

You'd find grains from a single farm in Hampshire, with two varieties of spring barley, Laureate and Concerto, selected for their efficiency of extract. You'd find those grains floor-malted at Warminster, where a highly experienced operative keeps a close eye on their quality as they are turned by hand while kilning. You'd find them mashed in wooden tuns at a slightly higher temperature than normal, again for a better extract. You'd find the resulting wort fermented for a whole week – blessed by the Sabbath, as a brewer would describe it – in open wooden tuns for greater character, using a slow-acting yeast to generate fruity flavours in the whisky. You'd find bespoke hand-made Portuguese copper pots – Doris, the 1000-litre wash still, and Astraea, the 600-litre spirit still named after a Greek goddess of cleanliness and purity – dimpled for vastly greater contact with the condensate. And you'd find the spirit maturing in an array of sizes and fills, as many as the pipes of a church organ, not necessarily for years and years but until it is at its optimum. Yep, that's a distillery that shows all the imagination and openness that, unfettered by stuffy old Scottish custom and practice, can only be English.

Only, er... the partners who founded the Bimber distillery in Ealing, West London aren't English. They are architect/builder Dariusz Plazewski and designer Ewelina Chruszczyk, who arrived from Poland in 2003 and did well enough in business to set up one of the most complete artisan distilling operations in the country.

So complete that it even has its own coopers – well, joiners seconded from Darius's construction company, which is as good as. This insistence on control and self-sufficiency is perhaps down to Dariusz's discipline as an architect – a discipline that requires its practitioners to place with absolute precision every doorknob, light switch, radiator and power point on the blueprint of a 20-storey office block – and also as the third generation of a family of moonshiners.

Bimber is named after a Polish word for moonshine or home-made spirit, widely made since the mid-nineteenth century by the poor and the oppressed who adapted the cheap mass-produced ironmongery becoming available at the time to the purpose. For well over a century whoever was in power, whether Catholic or Communist, sought to restrict commercial alcohol production for one reason or another, and fermentable materials were usually scarce. Working-class home distillers, both urban and rural, used sugar and its variants including caramel and molasses as well as roots, fruits and cereals, especially rye, to concoct a wash from which they contrived as pure a spirit as their odd assortments of pans and buckets would allow. Batches were necessarily small, and to get a product of saleable quality and consistency was a painstaking affair demanding, like architecture, extraordinary attention to detail. This lesson Dariusz learned at his grandfather's knee, and this lesson underpins everything he and Ewelina have achieved at Bimber.

Like most English whisky distillers Dariusz got the ball rolling with a couple of gins, including one flavoured with kumquat and another with green tea. The first whisky was laid down in 2016 and released after 3½ years to very favourable reviews. Batch after batch has followed, much of the output disappearing into the hands of hoarders or, as they are dismissively described, 'flippers'. Dariusz doesn't mind, but he thinks that if you've spent the money you deserve to experience the pleasure. Meanwhile, Bimber moves on: a sister distillery, which includes its own floor-maltings, Dunphail, Morayshire is now open to visitors; and the original distillery itself will shortly be on the move to new premises. This will be a great relief to its fans since the current venue, although warm and welcoming to tasters and tourists, is in one of London's less prepossessing localities: the light industrial estate at Park Royal.

Dariusz Plazewski has now relinquished all his responsibilities for both Bimber and Dunphail distilleries and is handing over all decision-making and operational matters to Co-Founder Ewelina Chruszczyk and Dunphail Director of Whisky Creation, Matt McKay.

 TASTING NOTES

Bimber Oloroso Cask Batch 2, 51.7% abv

Nose: Fruit loaf and raisins, toast and fresh pastry with sweet wafts of apple.

Palate: All the sherry! Deep, dark, rich dried fruit flavours, caramelised nuts and gentle cakey spice.

Finish: Syrup and honey poured over tropical fruit, gentle cinnamon and allspice.

DOGHOUSE DISTILLERY

📍 *Unit L London Stone Business Estate, Broughton St, SW8 3QR*
🖥 *doghousedistillery.com*
📞 *0207 622 9980*
💬 *Number 19 on map*

Loosely inspired by various genres of popular music, mainly from the Deep South, Doghouse is a funky gin and vodka distillery in happening Battersea. Don't be fooled by the neo-hipster coating, though: inside is a fully functioning hardcore operation that mills its own malt, brews its own wash and distils its own base spirit.

Australian founder Braden Saunders is not short on genuine innovation: try the bacon and chilli vodka. Doghouse laid down its blues-inspired whisky – or should that be whiskey? – in 2021; so put some mournful slide guitar on the turntable, settle in and jes' wait.

EAST LONDON LIQUOR COMPANY

📍 *Unit GF1, Bow Wharf, 221 Grove Rd, Old Ford, E3 5SN*
🖥 *eastlondonliquorcompany.com*
📞 *020 3011 0980*
💬 *Number 20 on map*

One of the aristocrats of new wave distillers, East London Liquor Co was launched in 2014 by actor-turned-bartender Alex Wolpert and rapidly advanced on all fronts, guns blazing. Importer, distiller, wholesaler, bottler, bar, restaurant, tourist trap – East London Liquor Company has got the lot.

The chief or at least most immediate glory of the whole set-up, it has to be said, is its dream location in a hip part of London. Hackney has spent so long coming up in the world that you'd think it had reached cloud nine by now and here at least, it has. In the nineteenth century London was as thickly coated with industrial districts. London made almost everything it consumed and more, far more; and industry's various hives stood where they had been founded, however their neighbourhoods had evolved. The River Thames itself was lined with breweries, distilleries, vinegar and sauce manufacturers, jam-makers and all manner of sources of stink and sewage, even to its western reaches, until they succumbed one by one to the brown brick and wrought iron terraces of salubrious housing for the genteel. In the East End, the bombers razed the dockside factories and warehouses, to be replaced by the rather less salubrious concrete canyons of the rather less genteel.

To the north, though, many of the smaller industrial enclaves seem to have escaped the notice of both speculative builder and bomb-aimer, surviving to a great extent unscathed, their large and often lovely buildings ideally suited to the needs of a new generation of industry; and here Alex Wolpert found a canalside Victorian glue factory to be a home both spacious and gracious for his dream. As a bartender at the prestige end of the trade he had seen the public forking out huge sums for heavily branded and blinged-up spirits that in his opinion didn't live up to their price tags. His vision was to create top-quality brands at realistic prices because, as he has said, he doesn't rate expensive mediocrities and he believes that everybody deserves a decent drink.

In 2014 East London Liquor opened the doors of the stylish Bow Bar and its Italian-inspired restaurant, all bare brick and stripped floors and walled off from the distillery's twin German-made Holstein copper pot stills by glass partitions. But it very quickly got into gear, producing an ever-expanding range of white spirits. These range from a standard-strength gin and vodka at reasonable prices to the premium Lighter and Brighter gins and the barrel-aged Changeling, and importing abstruse and exotic spirits, especially rums, for bottling.

It also made history by laying down a whisky, released in 2019 and the first to be made in London for more than a century. Not just any old whisky, though: the wash is brewed on site; at 47 per cent abv it packs quite a punch and moreover its grist is 55 per cent malted rye. It has a more conventional twin, Single Malt, and brings out off-the-wall one-offs like the 600-bottles-and-that's-your-lot East London Blend, half rye and half Californian bourbon. Wowsa!

All the while, the company has been growing in other ways: it has shops in Borough Market and Covent Garden, and a global distribution deal with French-owned drinks business Mangrove. It also has its social dimension: there are, says Alex, enough bottles in the world already; so if you visit, just bring along an empty (and clean) 70cl bottle – any bottle – and they will refill and duty-stamp it for you. Similarly, the trade can buy a 10-litre plastic container which they can bottle themselves.

 TASTING NOTES

London Rye Whisky 2022, 47% abv

Nose: Roasted nuts, dried fruit and toasty spices with a whiff of red chilli pepper.

Palate: Apricot, black pepper, honey, dry oak and a smidge of floral sweetness building.

Finish: Rye bread with salted butter, plus hints of citrus lingering.

THE OLD BAKERY GIN DISTILLERY

📍 *4 Pymmes Mews, London N13 4PF*
🖥 *Oldbakerygin.com*
📞 *0208 829 8241*
💬 *No 18 on map*

Bowes Park's old bakery with its outbuildings including stables and grain store were bought in 2013 by entrepreneur Ian Puddick as a base for his leak detection business. Investigations during rebuilding turned up an old story that the baker in the late nineteenth century had also run a moonshining operation from the grain store. Intrigued, and despite having no experience of distilling, Ian decided to have a crack at it on his own account and, as the market was proving rather saturated, decided on a no-compromise superpremium operation, which soon attracted star endorsements from the likes of Joanna Lumley. Egged on by his customers, Ian decided to follow the gin with a whisky and now sells a small-batch eight-year-old malt matured in new American oak and finished in Cuban rum casks.

EAST

ADNAMS COPPER HOUSE DISTILLERY

📍 *Adnams plc, Sole Bay Brewery, Southwold, Suffolk IP18 6JW*
🖥 *adnams.co.uk*
📞 *01502 727222 (727225 booking line for brewery and distillery tours and gin school)*
💬 *Number 21 on map*

Dear old Adnams! It always used to be like a maiden aunt at Christmas: much fussed over for the duration of her visit, hardly spoken of for the rest of the year. Everyone praised the beers; trouble was, you couldn't find anywhere that stocked them. With only a small pub estate of its own it depended heavily for national distribution on the free trade, where its slightly fusty image guaranteed a healthy sale in prestige outlets such as (say) the George at Stamford but further down the social scale put it under serious pressure from the burgeoning microbrewing sector.

On a collision course with the future, Adnams seemed set to join other much-loved family favourites – Morrells, Mansfield, Morland and many that didn't begin with M – as stuffed heads above the mantelpieces of much bigger beasts' dining rooms. By the late 1990s its brewery had scarcely been touched since it was extended in 1970; and the brewery site, in the very centre of genteel but gridlocked Southwold, was a nightmare for lorries to get in and out of.

Adnams was rescued by a generational shift on the board that in 1996 brought a remarkable double act to the helm. Cambridge-educated, earring-wearing, food, wine and travel writing chairman Simon Loftus and public-school dropout, trawlerman and lifeboatman managing director Jonathan Adnams together set about rejuvenating, re-engineering and rethinking. They rebuilt the brewery from the inside, replacing old kit with new and adopting technical innovations that saved time, money, water and energy while allowing perfect quality control. Meanwhile, the management structure and operating procedures were reviewed to energise the whole company, and new beers such as Regatta, Ghost Ship, Lighthouse and Explorer that appealed to a more modern taste were rolled out under the Beers from the Coast banner. (Having said that, the old range including Southwold Bitter and Tally Ho barley wine were never neglected.)

These initiatives brought Adnams into the spotlight again, and output doubled; but once your success has attracted the attention of the predators they will start looking at you even more keenly. You have to keep moving. In 2006, the year that Simon Loftus relinquished the chair and Jonathan Adnams took it over, the company amazed the world by moving its distribution and logistics out of Southwold, sparing the town centre 50 lorry movements a day, and into a new building in an old gravel-pit. It's an ecologist's dream of green. Lime and hemp walls; sedum grass roof; rainwater management; solar power; sunlight management; naturally constant temperature... and zero emissions. All this technology was already out there, waiting to be put together. It was the fact that it took a 130-year-old British family brewery to do it that made the world gasp.

But Adnams hadn't finished yet. In 2010 it unveiled its Copper House Distillery, installed in a corner of the old brewery to make not only gins, liqueurs and vodka but whiskies of various types too, including Spirit of Broadside, an eau de vie de bière in the Alsatian style with a portion of its signature strong ale abstracted between fermenter and kettle as a wash. More than a decade after it started its clamber back into the sunlight, there seemed to be no end to the wonders it wanted to show us.

The distillery was the personal project of the new chairman, who attended a five-day distilling course along with the brewery engineer he had picked out as head distiller, John McCarthy. At first it was the old familiar story of having to put up with gin while we waited for the whisky. But again, whisky was always the goal. That doesn't mean that Copper House's base spirit is anything less than meticulously made all the way through from the grain grown on Jonathan Adnams's own farm to the glass in your hand. John McCarthy has even confessed to buying in neutral spirit (albeit from some pretty classy makers) for contract brands while reserving Copper House's own spirit for its own brands because, he says, it's labour-intensive and 'quite precious to us'.

 TASTING NOTES

Adnams Single Malt Whisky, 40% abv

Nose: Oak, bubblegum, apricot, moving on to vanilla and butterscotch and still quite fruity. After adding a drop of water there's kirsch and, yep, runny honey. Red and black cherries develop alongside a hint of red chilli and, increasingly, red rope liquorice.

Palate: Pepper and more bubblegum, white orchard fruit notes and blueberry with a hint of cookie dough.

Finish: More sweeties, a little spicy caramel and the cracked outsides of Smarties (but not the chocolate bit - that's to be found in the Triple Grain!), fruitiness lingers too.

As one of the country's leading independent wine shippers Adnams has naturally experimented with all sorts of fills for its new make. Of the three Copper House whiskies – rye, triple malt and single malt – the latter at least has gone into the sherry and port casks, and at time of writing is still fast asleep against the day when John feels the need to do some special releases where he might just pick a single cask and bottle it. He also has some maturing in tight-grained barrels, which he says, give more refinement but take a lot longer about it. Buy some now for your grandchild's 21st. They'll be rich!

THE ENGLISH DISTILLERY

The English Distillery, Harling Road, Roudham NR16 2QW

englishwhisky.co.uk

01953 717939

Number 22 on map

No-one can proclaim themselves whisky-lovers until they have visited The English Distillery: it's the place where a non-existent tradition of whisky distilling in England was reborn and when first founded was called St George's Distillery.

It's part of the mythology now that when international farming consultant James Nelstrop and his son Andrew produced their first 29 barrels of new make in December 2009 it was the first to be made in England since the Lea Valley Distillery in Stratford, East London, closed in 1903. That much is true. The journalist Alfred Barnard in his 1887 odyssey *The Whisky Distilleries of the United Kingdom* listed four in England: Lea Valley, two in Liverpool and one in Bristol. They were not, however, part of any bucolic tradition on the Scottish or Irish pattern but were all large, modern and extremely well-equipped plants. Mostly they made 'plain' or neutral base spirit for the gin industry, but by maturing some of it in oak (thus qualifying it as grain whisky) they could sell it to the burgeoning Irish and Scottish blenders. Only Lea Valley made any malt whisky, says Barnard, then contradicts himself by saying that Bank Hall in Liverpool made a little too. Tempting as it is, therefore, to fancy Nelstrop père et fils as the revivers of long-gone rustic arts, that wasn't their motive. Nelstrop Sr, as is so often the case with high-powered technologists and business people, had retired too early at the age of 60. He still had more than enough vim and vigour in him, and just fancied making whisky. So he did.

The Nelstrops could hardly have found a better place for it: East Anglia's barley is renowned for its quality; as Elizabeth I proudly told the Spanish Ambassador, Hertfordshire malt made liquor as fine as any grape. Perhaps as a tribute to the region's barley the distillery entrance is topped by a mock pagoda, just like one you'd find on a real maltings; and in a nod to East Anglian architectural tradition the upper storey is weatherboarded. The first release for sale from the imposing and actually rather handsome set of buildings came in 2009 and was noted for its delicate pale colour. Since then the distillery has turned out peated and unpeated malts matured and finished in a great variety of casks and bottled at either cask proof or 46 per cent abv, all to huge acclaim.

The distillery was always planned with you, the visitor, in mind. There are, of course, tours which you can book including the Original Tour, on the hour, every hour, seven days a week, with the optional extra of a two-course meal, the Ultimate Tasting Tour and the more expensive Create Your Own Whisky Experience. But if you just happen to be tootling along the A11 with nothing booked and no particular place to go, a swift detour down the B1111 will lead you straight to the distillery door where you can pop in unannounced for lunch or just a cuppa in The Kitchen, stretch your legs with a stroll along the River Thet and through the two acres of gardens, and load your car boot with plunder from the shop where more than 200 varieties of whisky are to be had.

James Nelstrop died in 2014. By that time, though, many other splendid English whisky distilleries had sprung out of nowhere, and yet more have done so since. So if he didn't actually revive a tradition, you could say he founded one.

TASTING NOTES

The English Original, 43% abv
Nose: Zesty orange, vanilla custard and grassy malt.
Palate: Nuttier than the nose, with notes of almond and hazelnut, milk chocolate and more orange.
Finish: Rich barley and a handful of spices.

The English Smokey, 43% abv
Nose: Cinnamon, smoked malt and blueberry muffins.
Palate: Full-bodied smoke, paired with light notes of buttered bread and peppery barley.
Finish: Stem ginger and lingering bonfire embers.

CENTRAL

ELSHAM WOLD DISTILLERY

📍 *Pegasus House, Pegasus Road, Brigg, Lincs DN20 0SQ*
🖥 *elshamwolddistillery.co.uk*
📞 *01652 686916*
💬 *Number 30 on map*

The result of a collaboration between growers Richard Arundel, Matthew and Emma Hamilton and Ben Mordue, Elsham Wold began producing its Dutch Barn potato vodka from a big purpose-built distillery (on the site of an old Dutch barn, would you believe it) in 2019. Potato vodka is far from unique, but this one is unusual in being single varietal. The variety in question is of course the King Edward, first grown at Scotter nearby in 1902 and named to celebrate the coronation of Edward VII; the vodka's official moniker is therefore Edward 1902.

The following year the partners laid down Elsham Wold's first limited-edition malt whisky, aged in miniature bourbon casks and finished in equally diminutive PX barrels. As soon as it was ready in 2023 the whole first release vanished in a flash through the company's Flarepath cask club; your best chance of getting your hands on subsequent releases is to join!

HENSTONE DISTILLERY

📍 *Stone House, Weston, Oswestry SY10 9ES*
🖥 *henstonedistillery.com*
📞 *01691 676457*
💬 *Number 27 on map*

Go to Oswestry. Not just for a day trip; for although Oswestry has its attractions, it has to be admitted that it's no Ludlow nor even Shrewsbury. No, go for two nights. Stay at the 4* Wynnstay Hotel if you're feeling flush, so you'll have plenty of time for a leisurely breakfast and a swim the next morning before you catch your train. Because there's vintage trains in this one, as well as artisan-distilled whisky and microbrewed beer. If you've left yourself time, and if you are that way inclined, you can have a quick pootle round the Cambrian Railway Museum in its 1860-vintage goods shed before embarking on the 1¾-mile puffer train ride on newly restored and reopened tracks to Weston Wharf and a splinter of pure happiness.

Weston Wharf is the other end of the Cambrian heritage railway and has an attractive little station (actually a brand-new reproduction, but a very good one) complete with café, community orchard and, right next door, Stonehouse Brewery and pub and Henstone Distillery. Stonehouse is a familiar name in these parts. The Parrs – Shane (an Australian, but we won't hold that against him, especially as the Stonehouse does Aussie BBQs, which are pretty bonzer) and local girl Alice founded it in 2007 and have achieved pretty wide distribution in the region. The Wynnstay itself used to be one of its stockists but isn't any more. Never mind: when you get back after today's excursion you can sample Stonehouse beers at the Bailey Head and the Tankard, after which you call in for dinner at Amber's Pizzas, which does the beer in bottles and also carries Henstone spirits.

The distillery-in-a-brewery concept by which Henstone's 1000-litre hybrid Kothe still from Germany, called Hilda, occupies a mezzanine within the Stonehouse Brewery and building is the result of the longstanding friendship between the Parrs and local couple Chris and Alex Toller. Chris has even worked part-time in the brewery. A whisky-lover approaching retirement after a career in telecommunications, he had always fancied trying his hand at distilling and it was the gift of a how-to start-up manual, *The Craft Distiller's Handbook*, that persuaded him of the project's feasibility. Planning started in 2016 and Hilda was installed on her balcony, queen of all she surveyed, in 2017. The wash was made in December that year and went straight into the still; the first release in January 2021 sold out within hours.

From a synergetic point of view it's a brilliant device. Keeping Hilda in wash makes the brewery more cost-efficient; expanding the product range to include spirits gets more use out of the bottling line (which turned out to be a lifesaver during lockdown) and sharing the malt order makes or should make for a bulk discount. In addition, co-operating in distribution creates the potential for new introductions for both parties; and having both a brewery and a distillery under the same roof with a bar and restaurant alongside makes for a much fuller visitor experience. But yet they remain separate companies, and perhaps it's the alleviation of stress that comes from the practical advantages of partnership without the limitations that can come with it that allows the Tollers to be so creative.

Which they are. Naturally they started with gin, but nothing run-of-the-mill. Their dry wheat gin at 44.9 per cent abv, navy strength at 57.3 per cent and barrel-aged rosé at 44.9 per cent were different enough to raise a few eyebrows, but there was nothing gimmicky about them. Nonpareil apple brandy is distilled from Stonehouse's own cider; there's vodka; a golden rum was laid down in 2022; and then there's Old Dog bourbon-style.

Henstone currently focuses on four expressions: bourbon, oloroso, PX and, rather interestingly, peated Scotch. Meanwhile, Old Dog is also pretty unusual, with corn and wheat as well as barley in the mash. It's the number of liquors to be tasted that prompts me to suggest a two-night expedition, but if you don't care to schlep back and forth between Weston Wharf and Oswestry and vintage trains really don't do it for you don't worry: the Stonehouse does B&B.

 TASTING NOTES

Henstone Single Malt, 43.8% abv

Nose: Underripe apricot, chocolate-coated nuts and orange loaf cake slathered in vanilla buttercream.

Palate: More oily nuts, with chocolate praline in tow and a zip of pink grapefruit.

Finish: A rich, malty finish.

LUDLOW DISTILLERY

📍 *Ludlow Farm Shop, Bromfield, Shropshire SY8 2JR*

💻 *ludlowdistillery.co.uk*

📞 *07592 580567/07928 621608*

💬 *Number 26 on map*

Whisky-lovers everywhere owe a debt of gratitude to Shaun Ward of Shropshire Hills or, as it now is, Ludlow Distillery; not just for his own achievements but for continuing and developing the work of one of the first-generation artisan distillers, Mike Hardingham.

A Bristolian by origin and a musician by trade, Shaun migrated north to the Shangri-La of the Shropshire–Herefordshire border country when his husband became organist at Hereford Cathedral and he took on the role of master of music at St Laurence's Church in Ludlow – a job, which included the post of clerk of works, which meant he spent half his working life shoring the venerable pile up and the other half shaking it down.

He still gives the odd recital, but his main occupation since founding the venture in 2018 has been running and indeed expanding the Ludlow Gin Distillery, which two years ago became, almost by accident, a whisky distillery as well. And by quitting the ancient town and trekking up into the wilds of the enchanted Clee Hills we shall find out how.

The idea of installing a distillery came to Mike Hardingham of Ludlow Vineyard, squirrelled away up in the evanescently tiny hamlet of Clee St Margaret, when in 2009 he sampled some 'very impressive' brandy from Moor Lynch Vineyard in

Devon. Being a Calvados lover, he originally planned to make apple brandy and to distil wine only when the grape harvest was low on quality or overgenerous in quantity. Having already been a winemaker for several years he knew the ways of HMRC and knew he had nothing to fear beyond writer's cramp from form filling. After much investigation he had a 200-litre pot still with a four-plate refining column made by Koche in Germany and started distilling both grape and apple brandies for himself and on a contract basis. Such a small but versatile still allowed Mike to create many other spirits as well as his own brandies – apple and pear eaux de vie, marc, gin and, yes, whisky – which, because of the scale of his operation, were all profitable even in short runs and turned a small business into a small-to-medium one.

But tempus always fugit, and there came a time – coincidentally, during lockdown – when Mike felt the urge to hang up whatever it is that distillers hang up. Then, again coincidentally, he ran into Shaun at a local event. They began talking, and before anyone knew it Mike had asked Shaun if he wanted to buy him out, still and maturing stocks and all, and Shaun had said 'I do'.

Before long, although not without effort, Shaun had merged the two businesses and moved into a new home at the highly prestigious Ludlow Farm Shop, which is so much more than any other farm shop you've browsed. It's the retail end of a 6500-acre estate whose beef, lamb, venison, rare-breed pork, dairy and kitchen garden produce it stocks and where leased units include a butcher, a baker and even a candle-maker – well, a coffee-roaster, but it'll do – a tearoom, a gift shop and Shaun. Ludlow Gin Distillery's range runs to Earl Grey, marmalade, elderflower, camomile and verbena variants, and it operates the obligatory gin schools; but it's the whisky we're after and as it happens we're in luck.

Ludlow now specialises in short-run lightly peated limited editions, slow-fermented, quadruple-distilled on a small column still, matured in ex-Speyside casks, and finished in a bewildering array of every conceivable variation of oaks, all sold under the Wardington's brand.

 TASTING NOTES

Ludlow Distiller's Cut #4, 42% abv
Nose: Medium-bodied with fragrant notes of heather-honey.
Palate: Butterscotch and crème caramel.
Finish: A touch of aromatic smokiness from the Scottish peat.

MERCIA DISTILLERY & SPIRIT LAB

Bishton Hall, Bellamour Lane, Bishton, Staffs ST17 0XN

merciawhisky.com

01889 529291

Number 28 on map

If you're looking for the heart of English whisky – for what sets it apart from other whisky traditions – then Bishton Hall, a former Roman Catholic boys' boarding school near Stafford, is as good a place to start as any.

Originally a family seat, the eighteenth-century Grade II-listed pile was sold to a local auctioneer when modernity and overheads caught up with the practice of incarcerating small boys in rural prisons out of earshot of civilisation. Bishton Hall made an admirable HQ and showroom for the auctioneer, but it came with stables and coach house and all the rest of the paraphernalia of Georgian and Victorian millionairehood. These were therefore let out to purveyors of all sorts of handmade goods – hand-knitted shawls, hand-thrown pots (why throw a pot? The damned thing's breakable!), hand-melted smelly candles, that sort of thing. Throw in a tearoom pushing Class A tisanes and you've got yourself a retail destination where the Audi owners of surrounding parishes can waste their substance on hand-woven throws. Fighting through all this frou-frou finery, however, you will find, occupying the old school laboratory, a very important project. A laboratory.

Bishton Hall's old school laboratory was Mercia Distillery's first billet when it commenced operations in 2020. Still equipped with the Bunsen burners and Belfast sinks that created the stinks and bangs that were once the highlights of the inmates' lives, it's now home to Mercia's copper gin still, Wulfhere. It also entertains the alchemical dreamers who have fun adding sorrel and suchlike to raw spirit and even drinking the result. But as in so many cases, gin wasn't really founders Jez Roney and Oz Horrocks's first love. They were bourbon addicts; and in between teaching tourists that you really have to wash wildflowers because, you know, there are foxes and bunnies and lorry drivers out there for whom the whole of nature is a toilet, they have been making whisky.

And what whisky! Jez confesses now that he regrets using 100 per cent rye in the 100 per cent rye whisky because although the bottling of four-month-old new make at 50 per cent abv is already sweet and spicy and utterly delish, the mash was, essentially, unworkable porridge. 'It will be ready to drink at 2½ years, but then we couldn't call it whisky,' says Jez. 'It will be better still at four years, and brilliant at five.' White Dog is another four-month-old new make, in the bourbon style and bottled with an accompanying choice of five splinters of oak – port, tokaj, marsala, heavily charred and lightly charred – so that the lucky winners (only 50 bottles of each, folks!) can age it to their taste.

These whiskies, though, have never even met Wulfhere: they were made on an iStill kept at a temporary billet in foreign parts – well, Cardigan across the border in Wales – while Jez and Oz find a new base for it closer to home. Jez believes that once everything has bedded in Mercia will be able to turn out – and sell – 125,000 litres a year. Big numbers, but, says Jez: 'We're not scared. Scarcity creates curiosity and quality creates repetition. In short, demand creates itself.'

So there you have it: a jaunty and self-confident disregard for stuffy tradition, a complete lack of propriety, no rectitude whatever and if it feels good, do it. That's English whisky if anything is. Stay fresh, boyz!

SPIRIT OF BIRMINGHAM

Not open to the public
spiritofbirmingham.co.uk
Not open to the public
Number 24 on map

It is very odd to relate that Birmingham, Britain's second city by a very long chalk, has only just acquired its first distillery. But what, I hear you expostulate, about Langley Green, one of the UK's best-known contract distillers and producer of the base spirit that is the foundation of so many of the lurid concoctions that masquerade as gin these days? Ah, well, you see, Langley Green is not actually in Birmingham. It is in Sandwell.

Spirit of Birmingham, is though, safely nestled in the warm bosom of Hall Green. Brainchild of the Dillon family – ex-chef and home brewer Anthony, his wife Xanthe, and his sister Joanie – it's one of many recent start-ups that prefer an iStill to a more traditional copper pot. The iStill at the heart of the operation here has been installed in the family garage for quite some time: HMRC was happy with it, Birmingham City Council less so, and the questions of change of use permission and one thousand and one reserved matters – oh, and Covid – meant that although the company had been incorporated in 2019 it couldn't start work until 2021. It also meant that the site was not considered suitable for public access; so no visitors. Still, Birmingham had its distillery at last. And by the end of 2024, it will have whisky as well.

Gin and vodka flowed from the iStill first, of course, because that's how the business works; but, says Anthony, the whole concept was founded on 'an enthusiasm for whisky, whiskey, beer, and Tim Tam biscuits.' Setting aside the reference to a certain chocolate biscuit popular in Brum, this is a loaded statement that is worth unpacking. Whisky/whiskey refers both to the family's roots in the west of Ireland but is also a hint that they are not constrained by either Irish or Scottish conventions. The reference to beer takes us to Anthony's professional and personal roots as a chef and home brewer. As a chef, cost and other factors in his choice of ingredients come a distant second to quality and flavour. He could get 400 litres of spirit from a tonne of standard distiller's malt, he says, compared to less than 300 from a heritage variety such as Plumage Archer or Maris Otter; but it's not a consideration.

More heretical still is his attitude to brewer's or coloured malts. Contrary to some of the most august opinion in the industry, Anthony believes that the presence and proportion of these malts in his five-grain mashes has a dramatic, even a character-defining, role in the finished product. All his washes, he maintains, are the unhopped precursors to perfectly drinkable beers; the whisky currently awaiting its prince's kiss is made from a hybrid of strong Belgian ale and Guinness (those Irish roots again!) and is the result of experiments with 12 very different mashes. 'Guinness by itself made a very good spirit,' he says (St James's Gate take note! 'A bit too dark, but it was fantastic.'

You will be the final judge of whatever emerges from Spirit of Birmingham's dunnage later this year, but whether you like it or not it may never be called whisky. The pros and cons of distilling in stainless steel or insisting on copper have been discussed earlier (see page 89); but as a brewer Anthony maintains that the metabolisation of sulphite to sulphate that copper affects is unnecessary if you pay proper attention to your fermentation.

'Sulphites are generated by stressed yeast,' he says. 'So don't stress your yeast.'

WEST MIDLANDS DISTILLERY

📍 *Unit 1, 153 Powke Lane, Rowley Regis B65 0AD*
🖥 *westmidlandsdistillery.co.uk*
📞 *You need to email enquiries@westmidlandsdistillery.co.uk*
💬 *Number 25 on map*

Don't tell HMRC, but Jason Lunn was a seasoned home distiller long before 2019, when he went legit and incorporated the West Midlands Distillery in Rowley Regis and Dr Eamer's Emporium and Distillery Bar in Merry Hill, Dudley. His family home may have looked all sweet and innocent from the street, but behind that demure door all sorts of ginny concoctions were coming out of the back bedroom, so please, please don't tell Customs...

Actually you can tell Customs whatever you want, they won't care. So long as you buy duty-paid base spirit from a licensed distillery and take out a compounder's licence (free of charge, no qualifying conditions and you can't be refused one), you can mix up whatever you like in your back bedroom or anywhere else perfectly legally. This is a provision that allows people like Jason to experiment and also sanctions the gin schools on which so many distilleries rely for a second income.

Perhaps it's Jason's long years of patient practice that explain the speed with which his businesses have become established. Dr Eamer's distillery bar operates a single 100-litre wood-fired pot still, Doris, which is as photogenic as it is practical. The main production site at Rowley Regis has an array of three pot stills on which an astonishing range of products is distilled – gins, rums, whatever – both under the Dr Eamer brand and contract-made for quite small private-label customers. So why shouldn't your local balti sell a totally unique bespoke vodka under its own name? The short runs possible on Jason's set-up make it possible, practical and profitable.

But whisky is where Jason's heart truly lies. The rivers of rum, vodka and gin that have flowed into his spirit receiver have, he says, 'all been in pursuit of one day being able to produce our own single malt whisky.' And that day may be here. At the time of going to press Jason's new make is not far off celebrating its magic third birthday, whisky's age of consent. Jason has been putting all his skill and assiduity into exploring floor-malted heritage grains, yeast strains, and fermentation techniques and oaking options to bring you a single-barrel malt he confidently expects to be full-bodied and fruity. Let me know if he's right!

WHARF DISTILLERY

📍 *2 Brackley Rd, Towcester, Northants NN12 6DJ*

🖥 *wharfdistillery.co.uk*

📞 *01327 368866*

💬 *Number 23 on map*

Earlier in the book we followed Wharf Distillery and its founder Laurence Conisbee on their wanderings around the south-east Midlands from Milton Keynes to Wolverton to Potterspury to the wilderness and finally here to Towcester, where it is now the most interesting thing in town. For until their arrival the most notable things about Towcester had been its dog track, a proper racecourse until the gee-gees side of the business went belly up in 2018, and the fact that Mesolithic remains uncovered beneath Roman Lactodurum suggest it as a candidate for the longest continually inhabited site in Britain. But whisky is much more interesting than either of these.

Wharf's distillery is quite interesting too. Laurence still uses the little hand-beaten Portuguese copper pot, Velocity, and worm-tub he bought for the price of a second-hand car (along with a gas-fired paella stove) all those years ago, and he still buys wash from local microbrewers. But in her new and much more spacious home Velocity has a friend to talk to, Marie, a column still, which has taken over responsibility for Wharf's gins and other stuff. Velocity still makes the whisky, though: the Solstice bottling has been described as: 'An intense nose of salted caramel and hints of smoke leading to a balanced and rich palate of toffee, vanilla and butter with hints of cherry, followed by a sweet finish.' Equinox was due to be released just after this book went to press.

All this activity goes on in a 1940s-vintage factory built as a general depot for the electricity board right in the centre of the town, just off the A5 or Watling Street, which was for centuries Towcester's principal *raison d'être*.

The original depot was long ago divided into two but still has plenty of room for both Velocity and Marie as well as a shop and tasting room, although as Laurence remarks, no warehouse is ever big enough. Its half of the site was previously a steel fabricator's works and was a retirement sale. This was something of a blessing because without being under any particular pressure the previous owners could take their time disposing of their old machinery while Laurence gathered up and installed his scattered bits and pieces at a pace that might almost be described as leisurely. The occupants of the rest of the site are perhaps even more interesting, being one of only two distributors in the whole world of frozen bull's sperm. Wearing his contract distiller's hat Laurence is making them a private-label gin. A cloudy one.

 TASTING NOTES

Fyr Drenc Original, 42% abv
Nose: Smooth with long sweet notes.
Palate: Subtle smokiness.
Finish: Lingering finish.

WHITE PEAK DISTILLERY

📍 *Derwent Wire Works, Matlock Rd, Ambergate, Belper DE56 2HE*
🖥 *whitepeakdistillery.co.uk*
📞 *01773 856918*
💬 *Number 29 on map*

West Derbyshire is one of those strange areas where nature is in the process of reasserting itself over industry. You must have driven through places like South Shropshire, parts of North Yorkshire or Cornwall, where the old bleached bones of mine and mill and quarry poke eerily through the thin soil, half-hidden by shrouds of alder and spindly silver birch. West Derbyshire, where the Derwent emerges from the Peak District and follows its wooded wind to Derby and the River Trent, is one of those areas. Long ago the power of the Derwent was harnessed for all manner of purposes from grinding corn to breaking stone to powering looms. Then water was displaced by the coal from rich seams just to the east, and nature crept back into the silent valleys.

Nowhere exemplifies this mixed character better than the old Johnson & Nephew Wire Works in the magical Shining Cliff Wood, the surviving stretch of a medieval royal forest just north of Ambergate. Built in the 1870s, the factory spun the cables that went into some of the largest and most significant telegraphic and bridge-building projects in the world. Now redundant, its marriage of nature and technology was enough to entice Derbyshire-born Londoners Max and Claire Vaughan to quit the capital's gold-paved streets to seek their true fortune at the end of all their exploring, and to arrive where they had started and know the place for the first time.

Max, an accountant and finance broker and a regular at the Scotch Malt Whisky Society tasting rooms in Farringdon, and Claire, a teacher, had achieved that point of balance in their lives where they could either stay where they were or reach for what they really wanted; and what they really wanted was this: two fairly small hand-made copper stills – the smaller of the pair is only 600 litres – but with their long necks and in their Victorian industrial setting they look rather imposing; a full-scale brewery where they use live yeast from the excellent Thornbridge, a local brewery, in a full four-day fermentation; and a strong connection with the locality where they had grown up and planned to stay. It took until 2016 to find the Wire Works, but they knew the place was just right when they saw it.

That strong sense of place pervades everything here. The malt is Derbyshire-grown; Thornbridge, the source of the yeast, is in Bakewell; the distillery is the headquarters of a regular community litterpick that keeps the Shining Cliff Wood (a world heritage site since 2020) shining; Shining Cliff is the brand name of the broad gin portfolio, and the gins are flavoured with locally foraged botanicals (and Bakewell pudding!); Betty, the spirit still is named after an ancient yew in the wood, and the many limited-edition whiskies are branded Wire Works.

Since the first whisky release in 2020 the Vaughans have majored on small-batch single malts, mostly aged either in ex-bourbon casks or STR (shave, toast and re-char) – for a lightly peaty house character. (There are also rum and port cask finishes, and Necessary Evil, finished in Thornbridge Imperial Stout casks, which is very necessary and very, very evil.) The rather elegant fluted bottle (scrape the label off one and you've got a decanter) identifies the whiskies as siblings, but there's a growing variety of small batches to scramble after and scramble you must – they sell out fast!

 TASTING NOTES

Wire Works Caduro, 55% abv

Nose: Orchard fruit leads with crisp apple and candied citrus zest. Sweet Pear Drops and buttery fudge follow, joined by crushed almonds, vanilla cream and roasted barley.

Palate: Layers of honeyed stone fruit and caramelised nuts are joined by hot cross buns, a touch of anise and chocolate-dipped orange wheels. Creamy malt rests in the depths, with generous charred oak.

Finish: Subtle peat smoke wraps things up, while sweet, creamy notes of vanilla custard counter hints of gingery warmth.

Wire Works Full Port, 52.4% abv

Nose: Cinder toffee, red berries, caramel, espresso and cinnamon.

Palate: Dark chocolate, marzipan, bonfire smoke, cherry and fudge.

Finish: Hibiscus and vanilla.

NORTH

AD GEFRIN DISTILLERY

📍 *South Rd, Wooler, Northumberland NE71 6NJ*
🖥 *adgefrin.co.uk*
📞 *01668 281554*
💬 *Number 39 on map*

Yeavering, all whisky obsessives will be fascinated to learn, is an important archaeological site in Northumberland, which has been the subject of intense diggings and scrapings since its outlines were revealed by aerial photography after World War II. Its prominence lies in the fact that it was briefly the seat of the Anglian kings of Bernicia, noted by Bede as 'Adgefrin' at a time when they were aggressively contesting the top slot with their contemporaries in Anglo-Saxon England. It had a short but adventurous life from (about) 600 to (about) 650; after which it mouldered away completely, leaving nothing but crop-marks. The site was never built over, so everything left on the ground gradually disappeared underneath it as decades of wind drift, leaf fall and animal droppings and carcases deepened and compacted awaiting the arrival of those first frenzied trowels in 1953.

Now Wooler, a small town, a few miles down the A697 from the site, has got its own equivalent of Jorvik in the Ad Gefrin experience, a £16 million bid to regenerate the town and surrounding countryside through tourism by recreating King Edwin of Bernicia's palace compound. A torrid five-year build, complicated first by Covid and then by materials inflation caused by the war in Ukraine, never daunted the founders Eileen and Alan Ferguson. Locally born and raised businesspeople motivated to perform mighty deeds by the economic plight of their native town, they finally got to cut the ribbon on 25 March 2023, revealing a somewhat un-Anglian but astonishingly beautiful covered atrium, a bar and bistro, a museum featuring genuine high-prestige artefacts on loan from institutions both local and national, a reconstructed great hall and a whisky distillery.

Made on two Forsyth copper pots from barley grown in the county and malted at Simpson's in Berwick, the first whisky is due for release in November 2025. It will be the first (known) whisky to come out of Northumberland since the Coquetdale moonshiners we met in Chapter 1. While the new make is metamorphosing we have Tácnbora or, in seventh-century Anglian, standard-bearer, a blend of Scotch and Irish malts chosen, in Ad Gefrin's words, to represent the Scots and Irish who would have lived here at the time. [Well, they wouldn't: the population of Bernicia was composed of the Anglian conquerors of the Brythonic peoples of the former kingdom of Bryneich and the surviving Britons of the former kingdom of Bryneich, who were still very numerous.]

But no matter. Releasing a blend is an acknowledged method of prefiguring (and indeed funding) a distillery's own make, and this one has been particularly well-received. It also makes no secret about its provenance: it says what it is and it is what it says, so you can drink it with a clear conscience and, indeed, with much enjoyment. The bigger question is this: no Angle ever tasted whisky, which was invented by Scottish farmers in the sixteenth century. So why is a historical visitor experience also the home of a whisky distillery?

Again, no matter. It just is. Wassail!

 TASTING NOTES

Tácnbora Batch 1, 42.7% abv
Nose: Poached apples, caramel and vanilla, with hints of white pepper.
Palate: Sweet toasted oak with barley sugar, orange peel and custard cream biscuits.
Finish: Chocolate digestives, nutty malt and honey-covered fruit.

COOPER KING DISTILLERY

📍 *The Old Stable, Stillington Rd, Sutton-on-the-Forest, York YO61 1EH*
🖥 *cooperkingdistillery.co.uk*
📞 *01347 808232*
💬 *Number 34 on map*

It is impossible not to gush when attempting to describe Cooper King. It is a box of delights: the place where advocates of a more eco-friendly drinks industry go to be vindicated; where cleanliness is indeed, in the environmental sense at least, next to godliness, where the woke can dream and the dreamers can awake. It is a place where every act, every choice, every thought, seems to be driven by a consuming love.

Of course, a consuming love of whisky and gin is not considered a virtue by everybody; but when it comes to Chris Jaume and Abbie Neilson then yes, it is. Besides, it's not only whisky and gin they love; it's the whole planet. Everything at Cooper King (it's a family name in Chris's ancestry) is lean, clean and green.

Respectively an architect and a biomedical researcher, Chris and Abbie took time out from their careers in their early 30s to explore themselves and Australia; and there they found not only themselves but also Bill Lark, the godfather of

Tasmanian whisky (the island currently has eight whisky distilleries); and in Tasmania they ate the lotus flower and heard the sirens' song. Now the early 30s are the most susceptible of ages: still young enough for visions, but experienced enough to make you believe that you can realise them; and so after a couple of years Chris and Abbie came home, heads full of plans and with a 900-litre Tasmanian copper pot still (in whose proper use Bill had patiently instructed them) tucked underneath their arms.

Home was an acre of Abbie's parents' farmland at the foot of Yorkshire's Howardian Hills, where Abbie's sister's old stables, disused and in need of repair, were to be converted into the distillery and shop. Only they weren't. A survey discovered that the existing concrete foundation slab would shatter under the weight of mashtun, washback and a 900-litre still; so they had to pull the whole block down, pour a new slab and rebuild from the ground up, recycling as much of the original woodwork as they could salvage. All of which Chris and Abbie did with their own fair hands (well, they got by with a little help from their friends, but still).

Their commitment to sustainability is total. All their power is bought from an ethical supplier, but solar panels are being installed for even greener greenness. Maris Otter barley comes from local growers (although it has to be trucked all the way to Warminster and back to be floor-malted), as are many of the botanicals including basil, raspberries and lavender for the inevitable gin. Others are locally foraged (and if you ever see a bunch of people on their hands and knees picking weeds out of a hedge-bottom, it's a sure sign that a gin distillery is lurking nearby). They have their own honey and have planted an orchard and juniper bushes as well. The one thing they don't do themselves is distil neutral spirit for their gins: they buy it in from a neighbour and macerate their botanicals in it, vaporising it in a vacuum still before condensing and compounding it all.

The one thing they didn't have at the time of writing was any actual whisky, although the clock was ticking on their first batch and the signs were good. Their new make at 47 per cent abv has been well-reviewed, and the couple are aiming for a full, rich and robust first release aged mainly in well-charred 100-litre casks shipped directly from MB Roland, a craft distiller in Kentucky; lightly toasted French wine casks; and casks from Tasmania, which we are not allowed to say have held port or sherry.

A final few words about that still. It has an unusual feature in that it's heated by coils immersed within the wash itself, making it as energy-efficient as a direct-fired still but without the caramel-generating hot spots. Does that make it an immersion still? Why not? It's as good a name as any. Oh, and it's entirely coated with the same microbeads NASA paints on to the noses of space vehicles to protect them on re-entry, which vastly reduces the still's natural heat loss and saves a packet in energy costs.

 TASTING NOTES

Cooper King New Make, 47% abv
Nose: Honeyed and very slightly fruity.
Palate: Clear, rounded barley elements.
Finish: Developing into softly spicy ginger and pepper notes.

Cooper King First Edition, 48.1% abv
Nose: Dried citrus and golden syrup.
Palate: Soft malt.
Finish: Warming spice.

DURHAM DISTILLERY

📍 *Prince Bishops Place, 30–31 High Street, Durham DH1 3UL*
🖥 *durhamdistillery.co.uk*
📞 *0191 329 3749*
💬 *Number 38 on map*

One of the most highly regarded gin distilleries in the North-East has marked its move to a new home in Durham's historic heart by laying down a whisky. Durham Distillery was founded in 2014 in the nearby village of Langley Park by former Teesside NHS CEO Jon Chadwick and has built its name on a range of gins that includes an 18-month-old cask-aged example matured in former oloroso and bourbon barrels.

The move will raise a few eyebrows: the distillery is on two floors of the Prince Bishops Place shopping centre, and part of the premises used to be a McDonalds. The stills themselves along with the visitor centre are underground, in a gallery that extends under the River Wear. The ground floor unit is the distillery's shop, which sells not only its own products but also produce from other artisans – beer, honey, coffee, chocolate, candles – in the district.

Jon was inspired to branch out into whisky by a tour of the bourbon distilleries of the college towns of America's eastern states and promises that the first release in or after late 2026 will reveal a light, smooth whisky accessible to a younger and more contemporary audience.

FOREST DISTILLERY

📍 *The Cat & Fiddle, Macclesfield Forest, Cheshire SK11 0AR*
🖥 *theforestdistillery.com*
📞 *01260 253245*
💬 *Number 31 on map*

The high, boggy moorland to the west of the Peak District is a truly magical place – wild, brooding, dramatic, like a single great frown. Even on a clear day – especially on a clear day! – the sheep that gnaw the reeds and furze look somehow precarious, loosely attached, as if a sudden wind might blow them clean off the land and into space. However sunny the day, when you drive over these moors you can't help but imagine them deep in snow.

The fact that the founders of the Forest Distillery, Lyndsay and Karl Bond, have chosen to make this magical moorland the home of their enterprise merely goes to confirm the suspicion that they are, in fact, a witch and a wizard. Lindsay was a beautician and therefore an expert in potions and lotions. When the Bonds started playing with compounding and rectifying in their kitchen she began combing the woods for wild herbs and such like to use as botanicals and – well, how witchy is that? And as for Karl, he was an IT professional, and they're all wizards anyway.

Before very long they outgrew their kitchen and rented a seventeenth-century barn in Macclesfield Forest to do their alchemy in and if you're not thinking Merlin and *The Sword in the Stone* by now you jolly well should be. Even their brand name and logo, Weasel, honours one of the little furry forest creatures that used to help the Bonds with the washing-up. Or is that Snow White? No matter. Anyway, the next magical thing that happened was in 2015 when The Cat & Fiddle, a lonely drovers' inn that had stood all hunched and brooding beside the Macclesfield to Buxton road for 200 years, was forced to close after a long struggle for survival. It joined a sad flock of old wayside inns ignored by motorists: the Saltersgate Inn on the moors near Whitby has had to extinguish a peat fire that had reputedly burned for two centuries and has been demolished to make way for a café and the Ram Jam, a fine eighteenth-century coaching inn at Stretton on a very fast stretch of the A1 in Leicestershire, was briefly the cafeteria of a service station that failed. A petting zoo and menagerie could not save the Plough on the A1M south of Biggleswade; and the carrier's cart for London has not departed the Wait for the Wagon at Chawston a little further north for many years now. A nobler fate awaited the Cat & Fiddle: Lindsay and Karl took it over, fitted two 500-litre pot stills in, laid down their Forest Whisky and then transferred their gin column into the same space.

At 515 metres above sea level the Cat & Fiddle is second only to the Tan Hill Inn on the Yorkshire-Lancashire border for elevation and is blessed with a labyrinth of reliably cool, dry cellars where the new make matures in – glory of glories – genuine English oak barrels made by a genuine English cooper, Alistair Simms, at a genuine English cooperage, Jensen's of Ripon.

The barley that goes into those barrels, naturally enough, all comes from a farm just down the hill, while the mash is fermented in open-topped wooden vats accessible to wild yeasties and other beasties, using peat-filtered moorland water as the mashing liquor. What effect the rarefied air at this elevation and the Englishness of the oak has on the resulting spirit is for you to judge; I have no doubt that it is magical.

Before we reluctantly leave the Buxton moors, there is one more piece of magic to be transfixed by: the bottles. They are vitrified ceramic, not glass, made by Wade & Co, porcelain makers in Stoke-on-Trent since 1810, so almost local; and they are, quite simply, the most beautiful bottles ever made. The intricate designs were hand-crafted by papercut or collage artists Sally Taylor and Georgia Low and, in the case of the whisky, are of 20-carat gold leaf.

If you are of the scooping tendency, Forest is one distillery you simply have to tick off. It has a bar and a shop and of course does tours and tastings, so the trip from wherever will be well rewarded. A word of warning, though, it's tiny, much of the old inn's ground floor being taken up by not one but two distilleries; so you have to book even the bar in advance. Opening hours vary with the season, too: if the weather doesn't want you craddying about up on its moor, you're not going up on its moor. So check in advance.

TASTING NOTES

Forest Whisky Blend 27, 47% abv
Nose: Chocolate orange, vanilla and a touch of charred cedar.
Palate: Fresh barley, honey, toasted brown sugar, oak and cinnamon.
Finish: Cereal, clove and cooked pear.

THE LAKES DISTILLERY

Setmurthy, Cockermouth, Cumbria CA13 9SJ

lakesdistillery.com

017687 88850

Number 37 on map

Soon after its official opening in December 2014 The Lakes Distillery became one of Cumbria's leading tourist attractions, with more than 100,000 visitors a year. Perhaps people were just surprised to find a whisky distillery in Cumbria – surely it should be a few miles north, over the border in Scotland? – but if that was the case the novelty has worn off now, and they come because it's lovely.

The distillery is set in the Derwent valley where the river leaves Bassenthwaite Lake and heads for the sea, in low-lying country surrounded by frowning fells that demand to be seen under snow. The distillery itself is like a little castle, though, snug and safe against the outside and all its dangers, its stout stone buildings ranged around a spacious courtyard. It was originally a model dairy farm, designed and built in the 1850s as a practical test bed for theories and experiments in agricultural efficiency, but it had lain empty for 20 years when in 2011 Paul Currie found it, bought it and restored it with whisky in mind.

Paul has a track record here. His father Harold, having retired as a very senior executive in the Scotch whisky industry, opened the Isle of Arran distillery in 1995 with Paul and brother Andrew as his right and left hands. When Currie Sr retired, this time for good, in 1999 Isle of Arran was sold to a group of independent investors. Paul stayed on for a while but eventually left to pursue his own dream; and he found it here.

The key to success in a venture such as this – as at Isle of Arran, which in some ways it resembles – is to be the best at everything you do. That's not just marketing hyperbole: when you've invested £6 million for starters, with another £4 million later on, you need to be able to count on a premium that people are willing to pay. So the three-year restoration of the farm was painstaking and original, with no short cuts – even the ironwork gates to the courtyard were designed and made by an artist, Alan Dawson of Workington, and absolutely astonishing they are too.

Whisky distilling was always the objective here, but like all start-up whisky distilleries The Lakes started out with gin and vodka while the whisky matured. The gins, Lakes and Lakes Explorer, have been particular hits owing to their locally sourced botanicals including heather, mint and hawthorn. Even the junipers are gathered on the fells nearby. While waiting for its own whisky to come of age, The Lakes has also come out with two blends of whiskies from all over Britain, The One and Steel Bonnets. Its own malt, Genesis, was released in 2018 and there's now quite a range to damage your plastic with.

For the visitor there's an upmarket shop and an elegant 130-cover bistro occupying the original milking parlour: it's bright and airy and has its own terrace and, unusually for a visitor centre eatery, is open every evening as well as during the day. It describes itself as informal but it's a good deal posher than your average pub and the menu, although pub-inspired, is a bit pricier too. You could just settle for coffee and cake or afternoon tea, though, perhaps followed by a riverside walk where you can also say hello to the alpacas. Guided tours are frequent: every hour, on the hour. You might want to book just be sure of getting a place, though, and the enhanced tours definitely have to be booked.

 ## TASTING NOTES

The Lakes Reserve No. 6, 52% abv

Nose: Juicy, winey red fruit, plump raisins and sticky dates, as well as a tart, hibiscus-like floral undertone.

Palate: Smooth and buttery oak, more red fruit, alongside raisins, sultanas and sticky notes of runny honey.

Finish: A fragrant incense note, with lingering drying oak spice.

SPIRIT OF YORKSHIRE DISTILLERY

📍 *Unit 1, Hunmanby Ind. Est., Hunmanby, Filey YO14 0PH*

🖥 *spiritofyorkshire.com*

📞 *01723 891758*

💬 *Number 35 on map*

Yorkshire's first whisky distillery owes its existence to the fact that the malting barley grown on the Wolds is so fine that it would be a crime not to distil at least some of it. So Jim and Gill Mellor, proprietors of Hunmanby Grange Farm and founders in 2000 of Wold Top Brewery, decided to correct the omission. Planning started in 2011 when they teamed up with old friends David and Rachel Thompson, recruited the legendary consultant the late Dr Jim Swan, installed two big Forsyth copper pots and a four-plate column in a unit on a rather forbidding industrial estate, and in May 2016 flicked the 'on' switch. And in due course, after well-received releases of new make, along came a family of whiskies under the Filey Bay brand. There was Filey Bay Flagship, Filey Bay Double Oak, Filey Bay Moscatel Finish, STR finish and a series of limited editions all matured using different marriages, oakings and techniques.

What marks Spirit of Yorkshire out, as much as the quality of the products, is the love of the East Yorkshire landscape that has gone into them. The whole of the east coast of Great Britain, right up to the northernmost tip of Scotland, shares a mild maritime climate with the perfect soil and sunshine for growing malting barley; and the Mellors make the most of it with the tender loving care they lavish on their 600 acres. They use cover crops and direct drill rather than ploughing, both to maintain the structure of their soil and maximise carbon capture. They use hedges and streams to stabilise their soil and prevent flooding. They leave plenty of space for pollinating insects and the wildlife that depends on them; and they power the whole operation with their own wind turbine.

Wold Top Brewery is still there and still turning out some highly regarded beers, but as a separate sister company. Also on site is the Pot Still Café, which has become something of an attraction in its own right in a tourist area with plenty of competition. Tours are often booked out well in advance, and the evening live music and other events are a big draw with locals and tourists alike.

 TASTING NOTES

Filey Bay Flagship, 46% abv
Nose: Peach, apricot, buttered crackers and a hint of mint leaf.
Palate: Chocolate chip cookies, maple syrup, barley, more peach, honeycomb and walnut.
Finish: Gingerbread, orange peel, very slightly floral.

WEETWOOD DISTILLERY & BREWERY

📍 *Common Lane, Kelsall, Cheshire CW6 0PY*
🖥 *weetwoodales.co.uk*
📞 *01829 752377*
💬 *Number 32 on map*

Weetwood – the brewery in Cheshire, that is, not the district of Leeds – started life as a beneficiary of one of the greatest upheavals in modern pub history. The 1990 Beer Orders were enacted after a grand Monopolies Commission investigation into the nation's beer supply. The upshot of all the kerfuffle, after much strident argumentation and many a ramification, was that all the tenants and lessees of the biggest breweries – amounting to around half of the country's pubs – were allowed to stock one cask-conditioned guest ale of their choice.

Even given the number of pubs involved this seemed, to many small independents, no more than the crumbs from the rich man's table. But for newcomers like Weetwood, born in a barn in 1992 thanks to the efforts of two blokes who just fancied a decent pint and reckoned they weren't alone, the scraps of market space grudgingly surrendered by regional overlord Greenall Whitley amounted to a living. Thirty years later Greenall Whitley and its beer brands are scarcely even memories (the barley wine and Wem Pale were classics, the rest meh), and the Greenall Whitley names have even been dropped. (Although Greenall's Warrington distillery of Vladivar vodka fame survives and thrives, albeit under the rather drab name G&J Distillers.)

Weetwood, though... well, there was a generational change in 2014 when founders Adrian Slater and Roger Langford retired and were bought out by the McLaughlin family. Other than that, not much changed. The brewery's unusually wide and characterful range of session- and mid-strength cask ales continued to win trade accounts and customers throughout the region despite the absence of souring bacilli, exotic fruits and beer botanicals such as coriander and angelica.

Oh, except (that is) that the brewery has moved from its original barn to a much bigger home in Kelsall; a huge extension housing offices, expanded shop and tasting room has been added; and in 2018 the company sprouted a custom-made 400-litre copper pot still. As you do. Or as you did in the 20-teens, at any rate.

For Weetwood's expansion into distilling was as timely as its foundation had been, 2018 being the last in a run of good vintages for new artisan distilleries, with Covid a yet undreamed of nightmare waiting for its chance to paralyse vision and stifle dreams. The timing, then, was right; but not only the timing. The range of gins that flowed from that little pot still was also perfectly judged.

Cheshire is pretty much two separate counties. The urban north has long been dubbed the Manchester stockbroker belt and is studded with the homes of international footballers and TV personalities as well as the usual crowd of dentists, developers, hauliers and other haunters of the golf course. The rural rest, by contrast, is awash with old or at least posh money. The Duke of Westminster, of course, has his 'country cottage' up there; and tweed-clad farm subsidy multimillionaires – the sort who call themselves growers rather than farmers and couldn't drive a combine to save their lives – lurk behind every outburst of topiary. These are people with high expectations, and Weetwood's conservative but well-crafted range (and all made from scratch) includes a top-notch premium dry gin at 42 per cent abv, with sloe, raspberry and marmalade variants, a vodka and in a rare fit of quirkiness, an apple brandy.

But it's the whisky we've come about. As is so often the case, it was the first wash into the pot when Weetwood opened, and the other spirits had to hold the fort until it got itself good and ready to bottle. From the still it went first into STR ex-bourbon oak, but 50-litre quarter casks rather than the 200-litre American standard. The hugely increased contact area between wood and spirit hastens maturation and is now quite common among artisan whisky distillers who need a product that's good enough to justify the top-shelf price tag as soon as it's legal – i.e. after three years. Finally, the whisky is transferred into European oak to finish. At the time of writing there have only been two releases, spring 2022 and '23; but if Weetwood keeps on the way it's been going then before long it will be as familiar a name in Cheshire as Greenall Whitley used to be.

 TASTING NOTES

The Cheshire Single Malt, 46% abv
Nose: Apple pastries, with some crumbly fudge, apricot compote and gentle heather honey.
Palate: Plums and fresh apple, with toasted grain and oaky spice.
Finish: Subtle toasted oak, with spiced apple compote.

WHITTAKER'S DISTILLERY

📍 *Harewell House Farm, Dacre Banks, Harrogate HG3 4HQ*
💻 *whittakersgin.com*
📞 *01423 781842*
💬 *Number 33 on map*

A long-awaited whisky from the well-loved Whittaker's Distillery, housed in a 1950s ex-pigshed in lovely Nidderdale, had just about finished its long oaky sleep when it was released in August 2023.

Jane and Toby Whittaker have been making small-batch traditional-style gins including London Dry, Navy Strength and Quarter (bottled at just 12 per cent abv) here since 2014 and their decision to venture into whisky was taken fairly early in their distilling career. Localism is a big deal for the Whittakers: the barley comes from their in-laws' farm, which is also in Nidderdale, and is floor-malted at Thomas Fawcett in Castleford. Oh, and tasting experiences (this being Yorkshire) are rounded off with a complimentary locally made pork pie.

But they have taken localism a giant step further than anyone else. Other distillers have journeyed to Scotland, France, Portugal, Italy, Germany, Slovenia and all points east in the hunt for their stills, whereas the Whittakers toddled exactly 27.2 miles up the road to that great regional brewing centre, Tadcaster. Here local fabricator Tadweld, highly experienced in the drinks industry, was more than happy to accept their order for two precision-built 300-litre stills. As far as I know this is the only such instance; but although England may not have much of a whisky distilling industry (yet!), it does have a vast array of trades from brewers to caterers whose operations have stainless steel or copper or other pressure-vessels at their hearts, all of them getting their equipment manufactured, installed and maintained by experienced and competent local fabricators. So come on, English whisky distillers of the future! When sourcing your vessels, valves and pipework, forget Google and hit the Yellow Pages, because there's a welder in your town hungry for the work and more than capable of delivering.

YARM DISTILLERY

⌖ *8A Wass Way, Durham Lane Industrial Park, Eaglescliffe TS16 0RG*
▢ *yarmdistillery.co.uk*
☎ *07764 947781*
☺ *Number 36 on map*

Husband-and-wife team Richard and Sam Marsden had been in the drinks trade in various capacities – mainly as independent bottlers – since 2008 when they started noticing a sharp increase in enquiries for their services from small artisan gin distillers. Intrigued, they looked deeper into it and decided it was exactly the right fit for their business. So they shoehorned a couple of 500-litre copper pots into their existing HQ in Yarm High Street, got their botanicals in order, and came out with a range including dry, navy strength, Seville orange, sloe, rhubarb and ginger and one or two more tasty gins and, while they were at it, started compounding some choice imported rums to boot.

Not surprisingly they soon outgrew their premises in Yarm and in 2020 had to move out of the village and on to an industrial estate in neighbouring Eaglescliffe; and to celebrate the moves they laid down their first single malt whisky. By the time this book is published you may even have tried it: it's made of Northumbrian malt and oaked in ex-bourbon casks. But it has also spent six months in virgin American white oak, which, says Richard, has given the new make a complexity that persuaded him to bottle the first release at cask strength, so that you can water it as much or as little as fancy takes you and get a different result every time.

CHARTING NEW WATERS

Here is a list of newcomers, none of whom has (at the time of going to press) released any finished product. But there is one thing you can be sure of. There will be more. And more. And more...

2024: Forgan, Blackpool, Lancs; Willow, Flookburgh, Cumbria.
2025: Ellers Farm, Stamford Bridge, York.
2026: Abingdon, Oxon; Penrock, Liskeard, Cornwall; Spirit of Manchester, Manchester.
2027: Maidstone, Kent; Pleasant Land, Aldington, Kent; Aedda's Farm, Adstock, Buckinghamshire.

SPREADING THE WORD

So who drinks English whisky? Single malt and Cognac connoisseurs certainly – the kind who come equipped with discernment and fattish wallets, the kind who love a proper wine merchant's but will also browse the top shelf of a supermarket, the kind who will always give a newcomer a sporting chance: they drink English whisky. But they are a fairly circumscribed clientele. English whisky needs to cast its net wider if it is to match the significant achievements of English gin.

If English whisky's consumers (that's you, that is) are anything like many of the distillers, you will value innovation as much as tradition. You will be youngish, perhaps in that brief interlude of illusory prosperity between the first decent pay cheque and the first baby; you will favour beards (often scrubby) and checked shirts (often loud); and you'll be as happy with an Irish pot still or an artisanal bourbon as with a Highland malt older than your dad. Description doesn't fit you? It does in spirit, believe me.

You will take delight, and rightly so, in your discovery of English whisky. But that in itself is not enough. You also have a duty to convert, to proselytise, to evangelise. Only bringing new lambs into the fold will ensure that the fold continues to thrive. And this is happening all around the country through the medium of local whisky societies with their distillery trips, their tasting sessions and their festivals. Their festivals? Indeed. A growing number of local whisky festivals are being staged by groups of enthusiasts as platforms where aficionados can sample new treats while neophytes introduce their virgin papillae to a new world of earthly pleasure.

Only in such a social and convivial milieu can English whisky embed itself in the everyday of distilled spirits. It is (still) so novel a concept and such an expensive gamble that unprompted experiment is frankly unlikely, and the sapling industry is too small and too impoverished to encourage trial and encourage repeat purchases. So pour your friends a snifter when they come round; stage a tasting in your home or at a suitable venue such as the rowing club bar (overlooks the river but is chronically underused); organise a tour of a nearby distillery (short straw drives the minibus); or hold a festival.

A whisky festival is nothing like the more familiar beer festival. For a start, the glasses will be smaller. It will be a much more intimate affair. There will be no mobs milling about aimlessly, for the drinking itself will mostly be structured as organised tutored tastings; there will be masterclasses; there will be discussion groups and Q&A sessions; there will be distillery stands; and there will be close co-operation at every stage between the organiser (i.e. you) and the exhibiting distillers. You won't have to buy the stock – you couldn't afford it! – except perhaps for the introductory dram included in the ticket price. The exhibitors will see to that and will recoup their outlay in bottle and gift sales.

The English Whisky Festival is held every November in Birmingham and is organised by Exploring English Whisky, which is not a consumer group like CAMRA, but a small commercial outfit founded by an enthusiast. Richard Foster really only fell in love with whisky in 2017 when he was a content editor with Diageo on his client list. Shoots for the Johnny Walker range (especially Green Label) and the Classic Malts selection dragged him into the whisky rabbit-hole and in 2020 he staged a virtual festival on Zoom with five distilleries and 50 participants. Another followed, and in 2022 came the first live show. It lived up to all his hopes, so a second was held in 2023 and there will be a third this year – details eagerly awaited. Richard also organises the Croydon English Whisky Festival held every April, so his year is agreeably busy.

THE ENGLISH WHISKY GUILD

The English Whisky Guild was founded in 2022 and their vision is for English whisky to be recognised globally as a respected choice for whisky drinkers. By combining the experience of their now 24 members they aim to showcase the remarkable diversity and quality of their unique whiskies as well as to underscore the tireless pursuit of creativity, inclusivity and innovation.

In 2023 Morag Garden was appointed as CEO and one of her first aims was to submit a geographical indicator (GI) to the UK Department for Environment, Food & Rural Affairs (Defra). Morag had previously been head of sustainability and innovation at the Scotch Whisky Association.

There will come a time when the titans of English whisky are as visible and audible as their international competitors – and indeed Cotswolds is, at time of writing, already close to its ambition of a facing in every English supermarket. But until that time comes, the achievement of English whisky's potential lies in seduction by word of mouth. So, get seducing.

RESOURCES

BOOKS/PERIODICALS AND ONLINE RESOURCES
Brewer and Distiller www.ibd.org.uk
Craft Distillers Handbook 3rd edition
The Drinks Business www.thedrinksbusiness.com
Imbibe Magazine www.imbibemagazine.com
thespiritsbusiness.com
Whisky Magazine www.whiskymag.com

WHISKY FESTIVALS AND SHOWS
English Whisky Festival www.exploringenglishwhisky.co.uk
Harrow Whisky Festival www.harrowwhiskyfestival.com
Kendal Whisky Festival www.kendalwhiskyfestival.co.uk
Southport Whisky Festival www.southportwhisky.co.uk
The Whisky Exchange Whisky Show www.whiskyshow.com
Whisky Live London www.drinkslive.com
The Whisky Lounge organises whisky events www.thewhiskylounge.com

WHISKY LEARNING
Edinburgh Whisky Academy www.edinburghwhiskyacademy.com
The Whisky Lounge runs a whisky schoool www.thewhiskylounge.com

WHISKY SHOPS AND ONLINE RETAIL
House of Malt www.houseofmalt.co.uk
Master of Malt www.masterofmalt.com
Milroys www.milroysofsoho.com
The Whisky Exchange www.thewhiskyexchange.com
The Whisky Shop www.whiskyshop.com

GLOSSARY

Abv Alcohol by volume, expressed as a percentage, has succeeded older measures of alcoholic strength such as degrees proof, degrees plato and alcohol by weight as the standard method of calibration across the world.

Alcohol A group of complex carbohydrates including ethanol (which makes you drunk), methanol (which makes you blind), sorbitol (sweetener and laxative) and many others.

Aldehydes Natural chemicals found in fruit and vegetables (including malt), some of which are desirable but some of which generate unpleasantly sharp aromas and flavours. Aldehydes are metabolised by long contact with oak.

Amylase An enzyme found in barley, which allows the conversion of insoluble starch into fermentable sugar (diastasis or saccharification). Destroyed by boiling.

Azeotrope The maximum possible purity of ethanol is 95.63%. At this concentration the boiling point, 78.2^{0}C, is marginally lower than that of ethanol itself and well below the boiling point of water, so further boiling will produce no further concentration.

Bilge The bulge in the waist of a barrel which enables it to be easily manoeuvered and also traps the ullage or lees.

Blend Mixture of malt and grain whisky or of different malt whiskies.

Blended whisky Most of the whisky we drink is a mixture of expensive malt and less expensive mixed-grain spirits, both of them at least three years in oak. Blending the two not only keeps the price down for the consumer, it also maintains a consistent product from batch to batch and, as with Cognac and cider, much of the skill lies in the blending.

bourbon Sweetish American whiskey made largely from maize. Since all bourbon is, by law, matured in new oak (an old trade protection measure currently under review) there's a plentiful supply of used barrels in which to age British whiskies.

Caramel Burnt sugar produced by hot spots in direct-fired pot stills.

Cask proof/strength New whisky runs off the still and goes into oak with an ethanol content far too high to be potable. While the spirit ages, a certain quantity of alcohol – the so-called Angel's Share – will evaporate; how much depends on the duration of ageing, the porosity of the barrel itself and environmental conditions, including humidity and temperature. It will still emerge at anything between 58 and 66 per cent alcohol by volume (abv), which is therefore known as cask proof.

Char The degree to which the inside of a barrel is scorched, usually rated from 1 to 4.

Coffey still A circulatory heat-exchanger in which ambient wash is blasted with steam, separating into its constituent parts as it condenses. Also known as a column, continuous or patent still. Can distil a wash of mixed grains to produce near-pure alcohol. Operates non-stop.

Convert See Amylase.

Cooper Skilled worker who makes, repairs and reconditions barrels purely by hand and eye.

Copper Malleable metal widely used to make stills. Converts harmful sulphites into sulphates (which sink) on contact. Also a vessel used to boil hops in during the brewing process. Derives from the household washing copper. Antecedent of the pot still.

Denature To contaminate ethanol and ethanol-based products such as white spirit with methanol and other substances in order to render it non-potable.

Diastasis See Amylase.

Draff Literally, waste either liquid or solid. Waste fluids that cannot be redistilled are either spread on the fields or go to make biogas; solids such as the acrospires shaken off the grain after malting and the spent malt after fermentation generally go for feed.

English Whisky Guild The EWG was founded as a trade association to represent and promote English Whisky. A majority of English whisky distillers are members.

Enzymes See Amylase.

Ethanol Alcohol is a large family of carbohydrates ranging from methanol, which metabolises as formaldehyde and will do you no good at all, to sorbitol, which is an intense sweetener that occurs naturally in some fruits and is a powerful laxative if taken in any quantity. Ethanol is the most benign of the alcohols and makes you cheerful and fun to be with, although perhaps not as much fun to be with as you think.

Expression Variants of familiar brands matured and/or finished in previously filled wine, spirit or other casks.

Fillings Malt whiskies used for blending.

Finish The transfer of a malt whisky into a different kind of cask shortly before the bottling stage.

Firkin A word of Dutch origin, a firkin is a quarter of a traditional bulk barrel and contains nine gallons or 72 British pints.

First fill The first whisky to go into a new cask.

Grain spirit Neutral spirit usually distilled on a continuous still made from various grains and containing only enough barley malt to achieve diastasis.

Grist The coarse flour or meal of ground malt ready for mashing.

Head Either end of a barrel. Both are called the head because the barrel spends most of its life on its side.

Heads The first running of the still, high in methanol and therefore either discarded or recycled.

Hearts The middle run from the still. The good bit.

HMRC: Her Majesty's Revenue & Customs is the government department responsible for regulating the liquor industry, among others, and collecting duty and VAT. It was formed in 2005 by the merger of the Inland Revenue and Her Majesty's Customs & Excise.

i-still The i-still was designed in Holland in 2012 and is a highly automated energy-efficient hybrid still, which can be programmed in advance and controlled remotely. It is relatively cheap to buy and easy to operate and is capable of much greater precision than most traditional stills.

Lees Leftover particles in the mashtun or washback.

Low wines Weak spirit after its run through the first or wash still. Historically the volume of spirit on which duty was calculated.

Lyne arm The pipe that connects the pot still to the condenser.

Maceration The practice of fermenting the mash without running it off the grist. Gives a much faster and more efficient extract but can create off-flavours.

Malt Barley or other grain soaked until it starts to germinate then dried, producing fermentable sugar.

Malt/single malt Malt is simply barley grain, which has been persuaded to germinate by soaking in warm water and then drying. This kicks off the conversion of insoluble starches into maltose sugar, which yeast can digest to produce alcohol. Whiskies distilled from all-malt liquor are referred to as malt or single malt.

Maltose The fermentable sugar derived from malt.

Marriage Transferring the spirit from cask to cask during maturation.

Mashtun The vessel in which the grist is steeped at around 67°C to create a fermentable syrup or wash.

Neck The copper chimney rising from the pot still in which the spirit vapours begin to cool. In a tall neck some of the vapour will actually condense and run back down into the still. This is called 'reflux' and makes for a smoother whisky.

New make Immature whisky, i.e. less than three years old. Sometimes bottled for sale but cannot call itself whisky.

Peat Supercompressed and waterlogged organic matter preserved in bogs and traditionally dried and used as fuel and horticultural fertiliser. Its rich smoky flavour also made it a favourite fuel (in small quantities) for drying malt, but the progressive draining and degradation of peat bogs has seen it fall from favour.

Pot still The basic single-batch still comprising a pot with heat source, a tightly fitting lid and a flue pipe.

Proof Literally 'test', as in 'the proof of the pudding is in the eating', the proof system was an early way of measuring alcoholic strength based on how dilute spirit had to be before it failed to detonate gunpowder.

Rauchmaltz Now that peat is so little used in malting, distillers can replicate the flavour by using small quantities of the German-derived smoked barley malt or Rauchmaltz traditionally used in brewing.

Rectification The process of redistilling either to infuse spirit with aromatics such as juniper or to capture and eliminate impurities.

Reflux See Neck.

Rye A hardy grain common in northern Europe, introduced to North America by Dutch settlers and often used to make beer and whisky. Confers a pleasant spiciness but tends to clog up the mashtun.

Saccharify See Amylase.

Single cask limited edition Whisky from, quite literally, a single cask.

Spindles Oak batons added to barrels to increase contact between wood and spirit and enhance maturation.

Spirit receiver The vessel that collects the spirit from the spirit still.

Spirit safe A secure glass panel between the condenser and receiver through which the distiller can see the spirit and make the appropriate cuts.

Spirit still After the wash has been through the wash still it is further refined by a run or in some cases two through the spirit still, which is usually a little smaller and brings the spirit up to cask-proof.

STR Shave, toast and re-char: a step in the preparation of casks.

Sulphites Naturally occurring antibacterials that work by giving off sulphur dioxide. Sulphur dioxide not only carries eggy off-flavours, it also causes reactions including severe headache in people who are sensitive to it. Contact with copper converts sulphites into sulphates, which tend to clump and sink.

Tails The last section or cut of the raw spirit contains fusel oil and other heavy alcohols and generally goes back into the still.

Tannin A natural preservative found in oak.

Terroir A concept familiar to winemakers in which the contributions of minute details of aspect, elevation, soil type, climate and other local variables to the character of the final product are thoroughly assessed. This idea is now spreading throughout the world of artisanal distilling.

Ullage See Lees.

Usquebaugh Modern form of Gaelic and Irish transliterations of the Latin *aqua vitae*, water of life.

Vanillin A pleasant-tasting antioxidant found in oak.

Vatted Obsolete term for blended malt whiskies.

Wash The unhopped ale from which malt spirits are distilled.

Wash still See Low wines.

Washback The fermenting vessel.

Wormtub An old-fashioned condenser. A copper coil full of spirit vapour passes through a tub of running water, condensing as it does so.

Wort How a brewer describes wash.

Yeast A fungal micro-organism that digests sugar, turning it into alcohol and carbon-dioxide. Both substances are poisonous and eventually kill their parent. The contribution of different yeast strains to the flavour of the whisky is only recently being fully appreciated.

That Boutique-y Whisky Company is an award-winning independent whisky bottler renowned for its discerning eye and eclectic range. They've carved a niche for themselves as independent bottlers of much more than just Scotch whisky, curating and bottling distinctive and delectable whiskies from distilleries all over the world.

The burgeoning English whisky category set an exciting journey in motion for Boutique-y. With a keen eye on its development, they've bottled whiskies from six English distilleries to date. This venture kicked off in April 2016 with their inaugural release from The English Distillery.

This initial offering was a 5-year-old single malt, a marriage of four unique casks between the age of 5 and 7 years old, which picked up a Silver Medal at the World Whisky Masters. In February 2018 they followed this up with another small batch bottling – a coupling of a peated ex-bourbon barrel with a Sauternes wine cask, which this time clinched the Gold.

Though not that long ago, these releases came long before the boom in English whisky distilleries. The English Distillery was possibly the only English distillery that had whisky available to purchase at that time, although the cider company and distiller, Hicks & Healey, had distilled some malted barley two years before the English Distillery, back in in 2004. Adnams started their whisky-making around 2010–11, and The Cotswolds and The Lakes distilleries both started distilling in late summer 2014.

One of Boutique-y's most identifiable characteristics is their hand-illustrated labels – these imaginative designs tell the tale of the distillery or the whisky housed within, each label brimming with humour, history and a generous dose of whisky nerdery. For example, The English Whisky Distillery label portrays the mythical battle between St George and a dragon, which is guarding not a damsel in distress but a treasure trove of golden whisky.

Their second English distillery release came from The Cotswolds Distillery in late 2018. This particular bottling was a union of three STR ex-red wine barriques distilled in 2015 and claimed Silver Medals at both the World Whisky Masters and the IWSC. The story of The Cotswolds Distillery is closely intertwined with the late Dr Jim Swan, an influential figure in the story of English whisky. To pay homage to his influence, they include subtle nods to him on the labels of their bottlings from distilleries in which he had a hand. For instance, the label for their Cotswolds bottling is set against the backdrop of an idyllic Cotswolds village, with a swan gliding down the river.

In 2021, That Boutique-y Whisky Company unveiled its 'Home Nations Series'. This was the company's first effort to really showcase the emerging whisky scene on these isles and featured several English whisky distilleries, along with one Irish, one Scotch and one Welsh. The ever-growing Boutique-y gallery was expanded with fresh labels for distilleries such as Adnams, Circumstance, The Oxford Artisan Distillery (TOAD) and White Peak.

Adnams provided Boutique-y with a delicious single malt from a single French oak cask, a testament to the renowned brewer's skill in applying their craft to the world of whisky. Boutique-y's label design paid a wry tribute to the stories of Johanna, a ghost who haunts the building's cellars.

Their Circumstance label portrayed a combined trading floor and distillery, where grain is swapped for cryptocurrency. The winged traders/distillery owners are a nod to the mythical beings which inspired the name of their sister distillery, Psychopomp. Embracing innovation, this 'whisky' was made from wheat spirit matured with oak spindles for 40 days, a process that imparts a surprising amount of character in a short space of time.

Another exciting newcomer featured in the Home Nations Series was The Oxford Artisan Distillery. They offered Boutique-y a whisky from their very first cask, a single grain aged for three years, and distilled from a mash bill of ancient heritage grains. The label portrayed a field brimming with corn, barley and wheat, with distillery staff diligently tending to the harvest. Set against a charming backdrop of the picturesque Oxford skyline, the distillery's unique self-built copper stills replaced the city's iconic dreaming spires.

Lastly, the White Peak Distillery captured Boutique-y's attention with their young 'whisky,' at only two years old. Matured in a STR cask, it's another release which bears the 'mark of the swan'. The label depicted the beautiful Derwent Valley in Derbyshire, integrating themes from the region's industrial past and the 2012 London Olympics.

With the growth of the English whisky industry showing no signs of stopping, we're sure to see more great English whiskies from this adventurous bottler, perhaps one day a 'Full English' may even be on the menu? Yum.

ACKNOWLEDGEMENTS

The authors would like to thank the help of all the distilleries detailed in this book and for the images supplied by the following distilleries: Ad Gefrin, Cooper King, Copper Rivet, The Cotswolds, The English Distillery, The Lakes, Penderyn, Spirit of Yorkshire and White Peak; and also the following: Neil Cooper 26; Florian Dehn 110–111; Getty Images 108; Steve Jenkins front cover (at White Peak), 36, 82, 90–91, 94, 113, 120; Chris Taylor 36; Warminster Maltings 73.